The Colours of Discovery

The Colours of Discovery

Volume 1
First Edition

Compiled by
Prof. Suresh Makvana
(Chief Editor)
Ankit Patel
(Editor)

The International Journal of
INDIAN PSYCHOLOGY

The Colours of Discovery (Volume 1) 2015

Edited by
The International Journal of Indian Psychology
88, Patel Street, Navamuvada, Lunawada, Gujarat,
India, 389230

Email: info.ijip@gmail.com | journal@ijip.in
Website: www.ijip.in | Helpline: +91 76988 26988
***

Arranged by RED'SHINE Publication (India), Inc
Published, Printed and Sales by Amazon (USA) Inc
****

CreateSpace Legal Department P.O. BOX 81226 Seattle, WA
98108 USA Contact: 206.266.4064 Fax: 206.266.7010
Email: copyright@createspace.com
*

ISBN 978-1-5169-5756-9
Price- 19 (USD)
2015 (First Edition)

This edition developed by Department of International
Publications, The International Journal of Indian Psychology,
Contact No; +91 9998447091, editor.member.ijip@gmail.com

Edited in India
Printed in The USA

Acknowledgment

First and foremost we would like to thank our authors, who have published with us. Total 114 authors are joining with us from the volume 1. We would also like to express our editorial board members, who have experts of Psychology in the world wild.

We deeply are grateful to Mr. Bhavin Patel, who have not only put up with its distraction of us from their supports but have helped us with comments, ideas, and friendship. We also thank the Sardar Patel University and Department of Psychology for their grate support and giving platform to us.

We are indebted to all of our indexing partners, such as Google, Amazon, WHO, APA, Academia, OAJI, Research Bible, Amazon, Google Play, iTune, University Leipzing, University Berlin, University Bibliothek, University Des Saarlandes, University Regensburg, Hochscule Hannover University of Applied Sciences and Arts, Wikia, J-Gate, WorldCat and many more.

We also are grateful to those people who provided world wild platform, who believe us, who connected with us, who are publishing with us, who suggest us.

Editors

Preface

The International journal of Indian Psychology (IJIP), a broad-based open access was founded on two key tenets, to publish free the most exciting researches with respect to the subjects of our functional Journal, and, to provide a rapid turn-around time possible for reviewing and publishing, and to disseminate the articles freely for teaching and reference purposes.

The establishment of this Journal, The International journal of Indian Psychology (IJIP) is an answer to the wishes and desires of many researchers and teachers in developing nations who lack free access to quality materials online. This Journal opts to bring panacea to this problem, and to encourage research development.

The International journal of Indian Psychology aims at to establish a publishing house that is open to all. It aims to disseminate knowledge; provide a learned reference in the field; and establish channels of communication between academic and research experts, policy makers and executives in industry, commerce and investment institutions.

This edition covers the abstracts which have been published in Volume 1, from 2013-14. The aim of this edition is to promote various new researches. It also includes the authors' work to be presented and promoted to the whole world.

We hope that our aim would be success. The Volume will open the door for new researches, which will be useful to several authors' researches, articles, and books.

We have tried our best to bring out this volume according our knowledge and experience; however, we would appreciate your suggestions, comments, feedback.

The International Journal of Indian Psychology always welcomes submissions that explore research in the field of Psychology, Social sciences, Education, and Home science aspects of human behavior.

Editor note

The views expressed by the authors in their articles, reviews etc in this volume are their own. The Editor, Publisher and owner are not responsible for them.

The International Journal of Indian Psychology (IJIP) provides platform for researchers to publish and discuss their original research and review work. IJIP cannot be held responsible for views, opinions and written statements of researchers published in the journal. IJIP strongly condemn and discourage practice of plagiarism.

Include all abstracts in the volume are related to Volume 1 (Publish in 2013-14) at IJIP.

Contents

		Page No.
Adjustment		
1	Psycho-Sociological Issues In Old Age & Their Adjustment	1
2	The Psychological Adjustment among Male and Female Willing To Take Divorce: A Comparative Study	3
3	Psychological Adjustment: A Comparative Study of the Joint and Nuclear Families People Willing To Take Divorce	4
4	Marital Adjustment among Serving and Non-Serving Married Couples	5
5	Does Marital Adjustment and Psychological Well-Being Differences in Working and Non-Working Female?	6
6	Adjustment and health care awareness among youths of Rajkot district	7
7	Stress and Sexual Dysfunction among Call Center Employees	8
8	A study of Adjustment Problem among working women and non working women	9
9	Adjustment among Homosexual in Gujarat	10
10	Effect of Personal Variables of Youths of Rajkot District on Their Adjustment	11
11	Health and Adjustment of High School Students	12
12	The Effect of Vocational Training on Social Freedom and Adjustment of Rural Girls	14
13	Marital Adjustment of Tribal and Non-Tribal Women	16

14	School Adjustment of Higher Secondary School	17

Anxiety

15	A Study of Anxiety among Male and Female Adolescents	18

Attitude

16	An Analytical Study of Attitude toward Sexual Behavior among Graduate and Post-Graduate Student	19

Behavior

17	Effect of Mindfulness and Cognitive Behavior Therapy on Conduct and Scholastic Problems of Marginalized Children	21

Education

18	Role of Teacher for Peace Education	23
19	Healthy Practices in Teaching & Learning with Information Technology, and Evaluation Method in Classroom	25
20	The Development of Distributive Justice: Does Type of Schooling really matter?	27
21	Academic Achievement of College Students and Their Locus of Control	28
22	University Entrance Exam Result and Preparatory Class Average Score as Predictors of College Performance	30
23	A Study of Academic Anxiety of Secondary School Students With Relation To Their Gender and Religion	31
24	A Comparative Study on Dimensions of Role Efficacy between Top and Middle Management of Universities in	33

| | | Rajasthan | |

Emotion

| 25 | Emotional Competence of Adolescents in Joint Family and Nuclear Family | 34 |

Emotional Intelligence

26	Emotional Intelligence among Professors of Granted and Non-Granted Collages: A Comparative Study	35
27	Emotional Intelligence as a Related To Difference Areas, Stream' and Sex' among School Student	36
28	Emotional Intelligence of Boys and Girls Studying In Undergraduate Courses	37
29	Self Compassion and Emotional Intelligence of Engineering and Dental College Students	38
30	Gender and Emotional Intelligence of Collage going students	39

General Issues

31	T. V. serial and Aggression	40
32	Adolescence at Risk: An Overview	41
33	The Age Differences in Training of the Holistic Living Life Style	43
34	Effect of Media on Children Behaviour: Media Psychological Perspective	44

Human Interaction

| 35 | The Science of Human Interaction | 45 |

Insecurity

| 36 | Peer-group context insecurity' in upper and lower class youth | 46 |

Leadership

| 37 | Leadership Style of Pharmaceutical and Engineering Company Employees | 47 |

Mental Health

38	Mental Health among Professor and Primary Women Teacher: A Comparative Study	49
39	Mental Health among Joint and Separate Family's Women: A Comparative Study	50
40	Mental Health for Lady Teachers of Government and Private Schools	51
41	Mental Health among Married and Unmarried Women	52
42	Mental Health of Working and Non Working Women in Ahmadabad	53
43	Mental Health and Marital Adjustment among Working and Non Working Women	54
44	Sports for Positive Mental Health: A Comparative Study of Mental Health among Individual Athletes, Team Athletes and Non-Athletes	55

Personality

45	Ectomorphic and Endomorphic Personality: A Study of Emotional Quotient among Women	57
46	Correlation between Personality Types and Colour Shade Preference	58
47	Personality and emotional maturity of depressive and obsessive compulsive disorders	60

Religious

48	Five Factor Model in Iranian Culture: A Psychometrics Analysis of NEO-Five Factor Inventory (NEO-FFI)	61

Self Concept

49	Self Concept of Aids Positive & Negative Tribal and Non Tribal	62

		Women		

Job Satisfaction

50	Job Satisfaction and Organizational Commitment among Public and Private Engineers	63	

Stress

51	Stress Management of Old Age	64
52	Stress Management among Teaching & Non - Teaching Staff	65
53	Depression among B.Ed college students	66
54	A Study of Academic Stress among Senior Secondary Students	67
55	Life Satisfaction and Stress Level among Working and Non-Working Women	68
56	Stress Manage by Yoga	69

Well-Being

57	The Psychological Well-Being among Joint and Nuclear Families: A Comparative Study	71
58	Psychological Well Being among B.Ed College Student	72
59	The Psychological Well Being among Hindu and Muslim Educated Unemployed People: A Comparative Study	73
60	Happiness and Wellbeing	74
	Effects of Personal Variables of Call Centre Employees on their Psychological well being	76

Work Value

61	Work Value among Married and Unmarried Person': A Comparative Study	77

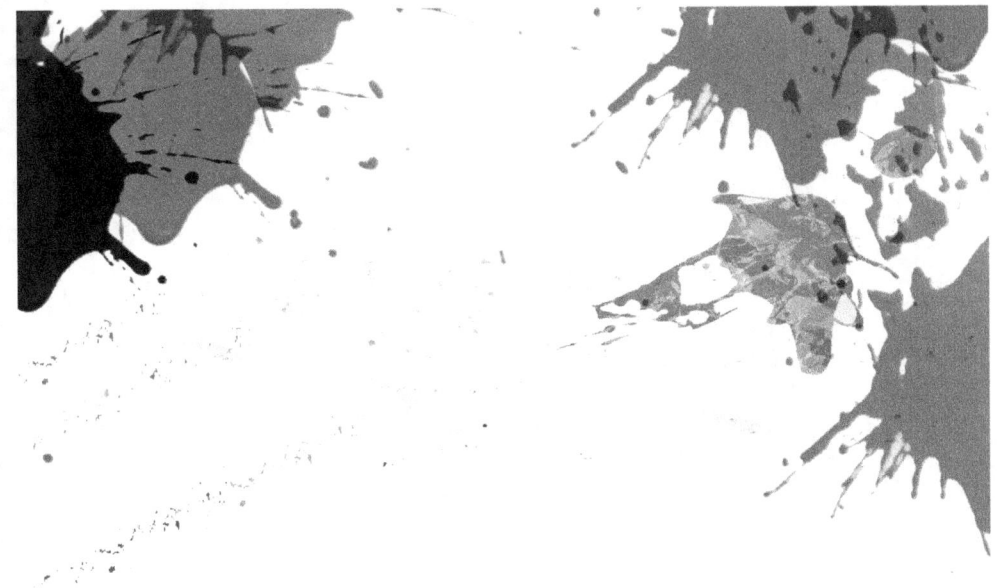

Adjustment

Psycho-Sociological Issues
In Old Age & Their Adjustment

Mr. Rajendrakumar M. Parmar[1]

This stage generally refers to those over 60–80 years. During old age, people experience a conflict between integrity vs. despair. When reflecting on their life, they either feel a sense of accomplishment or failure. Physically, older people experience a decline in muscular strength, reaction time, stamina, hearing, distance perception, and the sense of smell. They also are more susceptible to severe diseases such as cancer and pneumonia due to a weakened immune system. Mental disintegration may also occur, leading to Dementia or Alzheimer's disease. However, partially due to a lifetime's accumulation of antibodies, the elderly are less likely to suffer from common diseases such as the cold.

Whether or not intellectual powers increase or decrease with age remains controversial, longitudinal studies have suggested that intellect declines, while cross-sectional studies suggest that intellect is stable. It is generally believed that crystallized intelligence increases up to old age, while fluid intelligence decreases with age. For young people, time seems to have no end. But, as time passes we suddenly realize that the number of remaining years is limited. The realization that we are growing old can be traumatic. Our ideas about and attitudes toward aging are very important in how well we cope with and enjoy the passing years, Some psychological characteristics of aging get passed down from generation to generation through our genes. Others can result from real or perceived changes in our bodies as we age (e.g., mental or physical limitations). Social and cultural differences also affect how we deal with aging. Men and women think about aging differently, because of biological, social, and psychological differences between the sexes. For example, women tend to live longer than men, so they generally experience more losses of family members and friends.

[1]Assistant Professor, Shree J M Patel Institute of Social Work and Applied Arts, APMS Campus In Front of Near New Bus Stand, Anand, Gujarat, India

The Psychological Adjustment among Male and Female Willing To Take Divorce: A Comparative Study

Vikas K. Rohit[1]

Aim of the research is to find out the Psychological adjustment among male and female willing to take divorce so investigator selected two groups one is male and other is female, both groups have 160 peoples. In each group has 80 male and other one groups has 80 female. Data were collected from Anand district. Scale was use for data collection is personal datasheet and Psychological adjustment Scale was developed by Bell (1905) and Gujarati-translated by Bhatt, (1994) was used, 2x2 factorial design was used and data were analysis by „F" test. Result show, There is no significant difference between the psychological adjustments of male and female willing to take divorce. There is significant difference of psychological adjustment between urban and rural area, urban area show higher psychological adjustment than rural area. There is no significant interaction effect of psychological adjustment between sex and area.

[1]M.Phil Research Scholar, Department of Psychology, S P University, V.V.Nagar 388120, Gujarat

Psychological Adjustment: A Comparative Study of the Joint and Nuclear Families People Willing To Take Divorce

Sunil S. Jadav[1]

Aim of the research is to find out the Psychological adjustment among joint and nuclear families people willing to take divorce, both groups have 160 peoples. In one group has 90 joint and another group has 70 nuclear families people. The all subjects were simple randomly selected. Data were collected from Anand district. Scale was use for data collection is personal datasheet and Psychological adjustment Scale was developed by Bell (1905) and Gujarati-translated by Bhatt, (1994) was used. Data were analysis by „t‟ test. Result show, There is no significant mean difference of psychological adjustment between joint and nuclear families people. There is no significant mean difference of the Psychological adjustment between low and high age people. There is no significant mean difference of the Psychological adjustment between low, medium and high total monthly incomes people.

[1]PhD research scholar, Department of Psychology, S.P.University, V.V.Nagar-388 120,, Gujarat.

Marital Adjustment among Serving and Non-Serving Married Couples

Dr. S. M. Makvana[1]

Human being among living begins, has highest capacities to adapt to new situation. Man as a social animal not only adapts to physical demands but also adjusts to social pressure in society. Psychologists have interpreted adjustment from two important points of views. One, adjustment and the second lays emphasis on process by which an individual adjust in external environment. Married people need to adjust to each other, in order to live a happy life. Various factors contribute to the adjustment of the Spouses. The beliefs and religiosity level of each partner has its influence on the Marriage.

[1]Associate Professor,Department of Psychology,Sardar Patel University, Vallabhvidyanagar, Gujarat

Does Marital Adjustment and Psychological Well-Being Differences in Working and Non-Working Female?

Garima Gupta[1], Neha Nafis[2]

The present study intends to examine marital adjustment and psychological well-being among working and non-working women. The study was carried out on a purposive sample of 40 participants. Marital adjustment inventory and Ruff's Medium Form of Psychological Well-Being Scale was administered on forty working and non-working female participants. Results revealed that working and non-working women did not differ from each other on marital adjustment as well as on psychological well-being but on few dimensions of psychological wellbeing. The findings have been discussed in the light of relevant research evidences.

[1]Dr. Garima Gupta, A N Sinha Institute of Social Studies, Patna
[2]Student, Vasanta College for Women, Rajghat, Varanasi

Adjustment and Health Care Awareness among Youths of Rajkot District

Mohit M. Pandya[1], Dr. D. J. Bhatt[2]

The purpose of present study was to find out correlation between the youths' adjustment and their health care awareness. The said sample was 240 both males and females in equal numbers was selected through random sampling. Adjustment Inventory & Health Care Awareness Inventory are tailor-made instruments, having sufficient reliability and validity. For the purpose of analysis, The Karl-Pearans 'r' technique was used. Present study reveals the result that there is significant positive correlation between the youths' Adjustment and their Health Care Awareness. The authors suggest that there is a need to explore the rural and the urban youths' correlation in the line of above study.

[1]M.A., M.Phil, Department of Psychology, Saurashtra, University, Rajkot, India
[2]Professor and Head Department of Psychology Saurashtra University Rajkot

Stress and Sexual Dysfunction among Call Center Employees

Dr. V.D. Kasture[1]

This research results revealed that female employees from international call centers show high stress score and high sexual dysfunction than domestic call center employees, which means the female employees from international call center differed significantly (t=5.26, p=<0.01) than domestic call center female employees. Results obtained from t test showed that female employees from domestic and international call center differed significantly with one another on stress scores and sexual dysfunction. The reason is that international call center employees have more work stress as compare to that with domestic one. This due to heavy work load, not enough time for social interaction and completion of work within a given period of time. The work culture is more strict and systematic as compared to domestic one. International studies in the past have linked stress t sexual dysfunction and infertility among women.

The overall results of the present study suggest the need for stress management programs for reducing the stress and developing positive thinking among young female employees working in call centers.

[1]Associate Professor, Shivaji College, Kannad, Dr. BAMU University, Aurangabad, Maharashtra

A Study of Adjustment Problem among Working Women and Non Working Women

Kachchhi Parvati K[1]

The main purpose was to find out the main difference between working and non working women in adjustment problem. The total sample consisted 200 women in working non working women. The research tool for Bell's adjustment inventory. Here 't' test was applied to check the significance of difference in adjustment problem. The study revealed the working women and non working women were adjustment well especially from 'social, emotional and Health adjustment. The results showing that working women are more adjustment in terms of Health, Social and Emotional adjustment than non working women.

[1]Associate Professor, Shree Devmani Arts & Commerce College, Visavadar – 362 130, GUJARAT

Adjustment among Homosexual in Gujarat

Mukesh B Bhatt[1], Dr. S. M. Makvana[2]

The present Study of adjustment among Homosexual - female sex-worker, social men and women and AIDS patient from Gujarat. Total sample of 360 people was taken according to variables. In which, 180 male and 180 female were taken. In 180 male in 60 homosexual, 60 social men and 60 AIDS male patients and female in 60 female sex workers, 60 social woman and 60 AIDS female patients From Gujarat. The sample was selected randomly. Adjustment Questionnaire Developed by D. J. Bhatt (1994) used for data collection. The collected data were analyzed by F- test statistical technique at 0.01 level of significance and $2 \times 3 \times 2$ factorial design used. Results revealed significant difference between the male and female. There was significant difference in adjustment level found among homosexual-female sex workers, social men – women and AIDS patients.

[1]PhD Scholar, Department of Psychology, Sardar Patel University, Anand
[2]Professor, Department of Psychology, Sardar Patel University, Anand

Effect of Personal Variables of Youths of Rajkot District on Their Adjustment

Mohit M. Pandya[1], Dr. D. J. Bhatt[2]

The study was designed to investigate the impact of certain socio personal variables on the youths" Adjustment of Rajkot district. The sample consisted of 240 youths" (120 Male/120 Female) selected randomly from Rajkot district. Revised Adjustment Inventory (RAI) of Dr. Pramodkumar was used. Data were analysis by „F" test and„t" test. Results revealed that there exists a significant difference between the youths" gender and their Adjustment. No significant difference was found between the youths" Area, Education, Age, Type of family, Family members and Education faculty their Adjustment.

[1]M.A., M.Phil, Department of Psychology, Saurashtra University, Rajkot, Gujarat
[2]Professor & Head, Department of Psychology, Saurashtra University, Rajkot, Gujarat

Health and Adjustment of High School Students

Dr. Thiyam Kiran Singh[1], Sanjeev Tripathi[2,]
Prof. J. Mahato[3]

In this study random sampling technique was used in which total samples of 186 were collected out of which 72 were boys and 114 were girls with the age range of 13 to 18 years. All these participants were administered P.G.I. Health Questionnaire developed by Verma, Wig and Prasad (1978) and Bell Adjustment Inventory developed by Mohsin and Shamshad (1968) to find out healthy students and unhealthy students. The purpose of the study is to compare boys and girls on Bell Adjustment Inventory to find out any significant difference in home adjustment, health adjustment, social adjustment, emotional adjustment and overall adjustment. Another purpose is to compare healthy group and unhealthy group on Bell Adjustment Inventory to find out any significant difference in home adjustment, health adjustment, social adjustment, emotional adjustment and overall adjustment. The result found no significant between boys and girls in the domains of Bell Adjustment Inventory: home adjustment, health adjustment, social adjustment, emotional adjustment and overall adjustment. Where as the result found significant in comparison between healthy students and unhealthy students in all the domains of Bell Adjustment Inventory: home adjustment, health adjustment, social adjustment, emotional adjustment and overall adjustment which signifies that healthy students were adjusted well in all the domains of Bell Adjustment Inventory mentioned above.

[1]Assistant Professor, Dept. of Psychology, AIBAS, Amity University, Rajasthan.
[2]Consultant Clinical Psychologist, Greater kailash Hospital, Indore.
[3]Dept. Of Clinical Psychology, Post Graduate Institute of Behavioural and Allied Sciences, Raipur (C.G).

The Effect of Vocational Training on Social Freedom and Adjustment of Rural Girls

Dr. Javnika Sheth[1]

The main aim of the present research was to study and compare social freedom and adjustment among college girls belonging general and reserved category in rural areas. In this study my target sample was college girls. The reason for selecting college girls in rural area was to know their psychological attributes and analyzed it to discover important aspect of their personality and find out if the vocational training as extra- curricular activities, improve their social freedom and adjustment or not; that could be useful and meaningful for their future. To fulfill the motto of research, the Women social freedom scale –By L. I. Bhusan and Adjustment Inventory for college students- By A. K. P. Sinha and R. P. Singh was used. The random sampling technique was used in the selection of the sample for the present research. The sample further divided in to two groups. One is N1=60 girls from general category and N2=60 girls from reserved category (ST/SC/OBC). Thus, the total N = 120. Sample was taken from various college of Rural areas from Kheda district. The entire subject was in the age group of 16 to 25 years married or unmarried girls. They are from joint family or nuclear family. The pre-test and post-test method was applied. After pre test, I gave them vocational training (Beauty parlor) for three months as their income generation activities in future and then post test was given to all girls. The difference of the score of the pre-test and post-test was measured. The hypothesis was that vocational training will not increase their social freedom and adjustment. The result shows that there is the significant difference between their social freedom and adjustment after training. Their social freedom and adjustment level was increase after three months vocational training. The hypothesis was significant at .01 levels.

[1]H.O.D in Psychology, Shah K S Arts and V M Parekh-Commerce College, Kapadwanj, Kheda, Gujarat, India

Marital Adjustment of Tribal and Non-Tribal Women

Rathod Chirag R.[1], Patel Hiren[2]

The present study related to Adjustment level of Tribal and non Tribal Total 120 Marital's were selected randomly from Panchmahal district area's randomly. In which 60 marital (30 women aged 21 to 30 year and 30 women aged 31 to 40 year) from Tribal and also 60 marital (30 women aged 21 to 30 years and 30 women aged 31 t0 40 year) from non tribal.

After analysis was done according to key for the comparison of difference group 't' test was calculated.

[1]&[2], M.A. Clinical Psychology, S.P.University, VallabhVidyanagar, Gujarat

School Adjustment of Higher Secondary School

Chauhan Ajay.J[1], Maniya Anil A[2]

The present study was School Adjustment level of Arts and Science students. Total 120 students were selected randomly BHAVNAGAR district area's schools. In which 60 students (30 male and 30 females) from Arts faculty and 60 student (30 male and 30 females) from Science faculty.

After analysis was done according to key for the comparison of difference group 't' test was calculated.

[1]&[2], MA, Psychology. Sardar Patel University, Vidhyanagar, Gujarat, INDIA

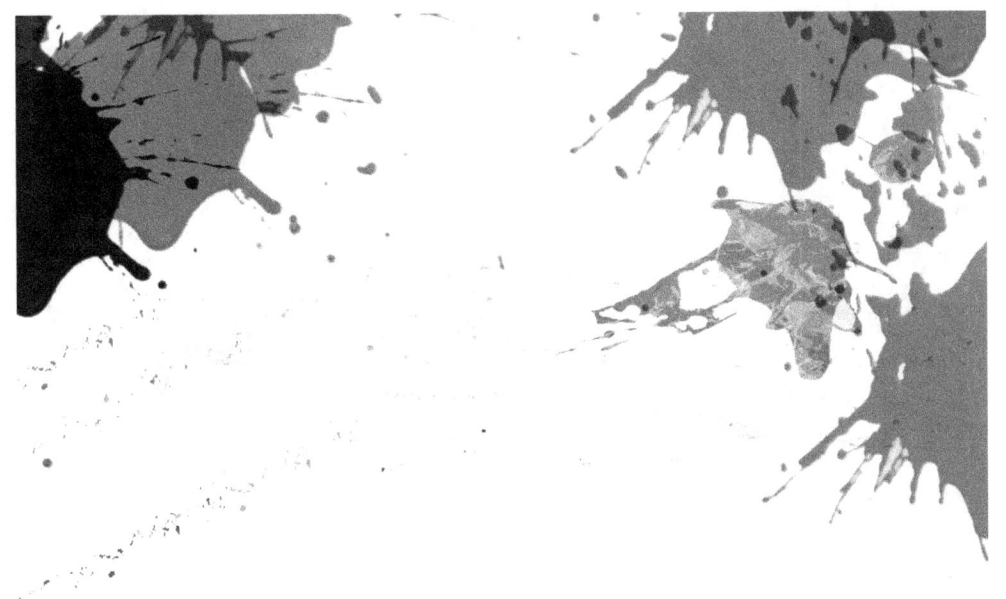

Anxiety

A Study of Anxiety among Male and Female Adolescents

A. K. Chaudhary[1], Deepika Jain[2]

The purpose of the present study was to find out the level of Anxiety among male and female adolescents. The local of the study was confined of Udaipur city of Rajasthan. The sample consisted of 60 subjects divided into two groups, 30 Male and 30 Female adolescents. Test anxiety scale by Dr. V. P Sharma (1971) was used to collect data. Mean, S.D and „t‟ test was calculated to analyze the data. Result showed that male adolescents have higher anxiety in comparison to female adolescents.

[1]Senior Lecturer, Department of Psychology, Govt. M.G. College, Udaipur (Raj.) INDIA
[2]Research Scholar Dept. of Psychology, Mewar University, Chittorgarh (Raj.) INDIA

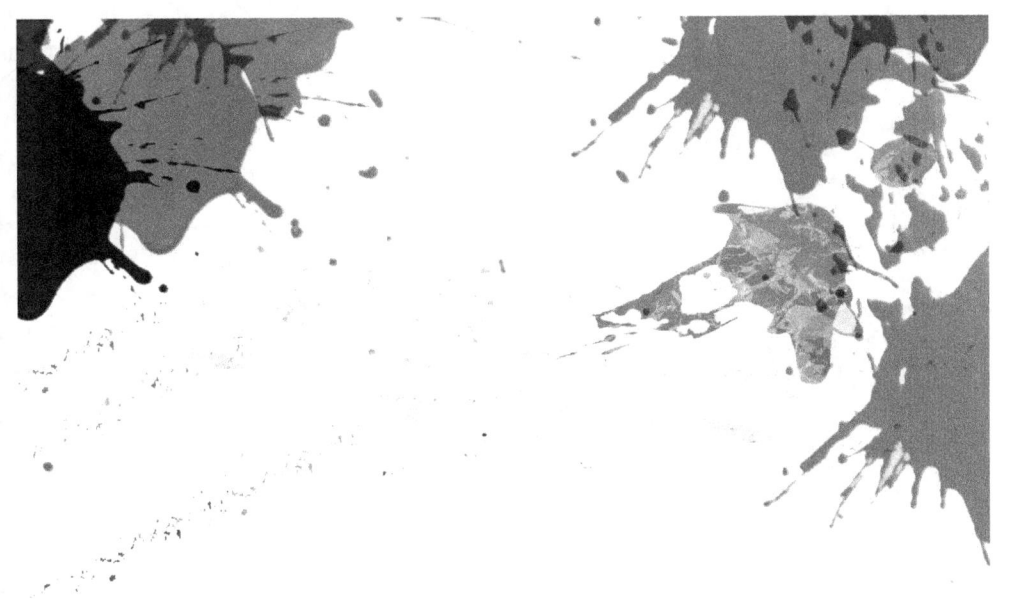

Attitude

An Analytical Study of Attitude toward Sexual Behavior among Graduate and Post-Graduate Student

Pancholi Haresh[1]

In present investigation the man object was know the attitude of toward sexual behavior among graduate and post-graduate student. 2x2x2 by factorial design by the use for the data collection, the scale of Dr. yashvirsinh was translated and standardize and used total 240 was randomly and stratified collected from the science college and arts college in Bhavnagar university. Further they were stratified of the basic of graduate and post graduate and male- female. The statistical analysis the „F" test for use the conclusion showed that the different of attitude toward sexual behavior was from significant between graduate and post graduate student (F=183). The different of attitude toward sexual behavior was from significant between male and female student (F=22.99). The different of attitude toward sexual behavior was found not significant between science stream and arts stream(F=1.32). The different of attitude toward sexual behavior was significant between education level and sex (1281.00). The different of attitude between sexual behavior was from significant 00.5 level between sex and stream (F=5.43). The different of attitude toward sexual behavior was found not significant between education level and stream

(F=1.96). The different of attitude toward sexual behavior was found not significant between education level, gender and stream (F=1.47).

[1]Vyakhyata Sahayak : M.N.College, Visnagar, Dist; Mehsana, Gujarat

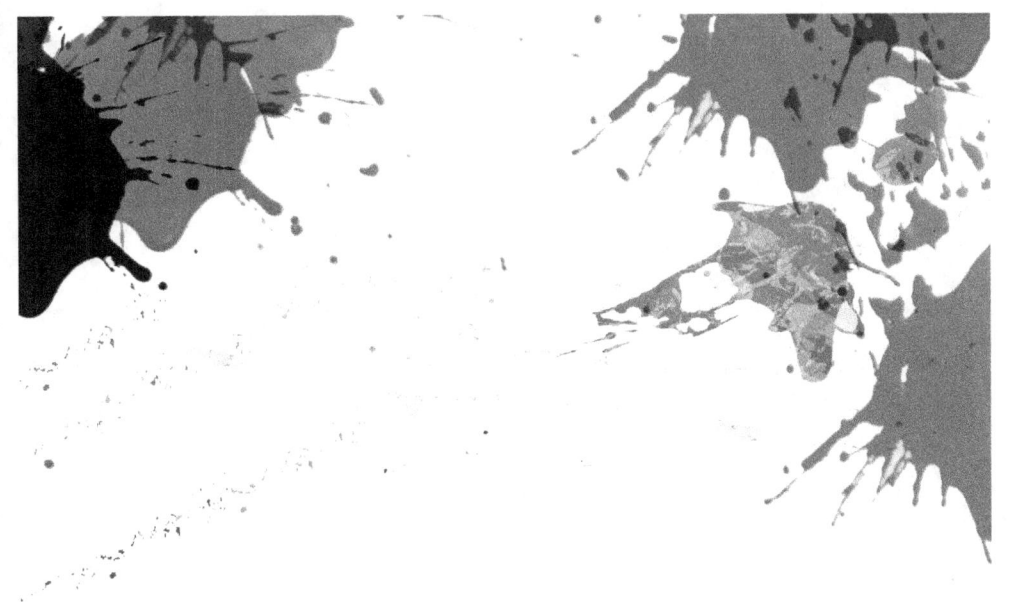

Behavior

Effect of Mindfulness and Cognitive Behavior Therapy on Conduct and Scholastic Problems of Marginalized Children

Dr. D. S. Charan[1]

The Purpose of the study is to measure Intelligence ability and social intelligence of students and thus we know that where should they stand in world of today and prepare them for World of Tomorrow. For this researcher has decided to Organize standardize social intelligence test for study interaction measures of Intelligent ability and social intelligent on scholastic achievement for standard IX students of Dahod Taluka, in Dahod District.

Intelligence is a property of mind that encompasses many related abilities such is the capacities to reason to plan, to solve problems, to think abstractly, to comprehend ideas, to use languages and to learn. Even in some cases intelligence may include traits such as creativity, personality, character knowledge or wisdom.
Types of Intelligence is classification are made by „Thorndike (1927) (a) Concrete Intelligence (b) Abstract Intelligence c) social Intelligence

According to spearman (1923), "Intelligence is which involves mainly the education of relations and correlation" Are all people equally intelligent? Are all the students fit for school instruction? No, But only some persons are intelligent, they Stands First in Class exam and they will some more marks.

Schooling is an important factors that affecting intelligence. Children who do not attend school or who attend intermittently score more poorly on IQ tests than those who attend regularly and Children who move from low quality schools to high quality school tend to show improvement in I.Q. Besides transmitting information to students directly, school teach problem solving, abstract thinking and how to question attention all skills required on IQ tests.

[1]Y. S. Arts & K. S. Shah Commerce College, Devgadh Baria, Dist.Dahod (Gujarat)

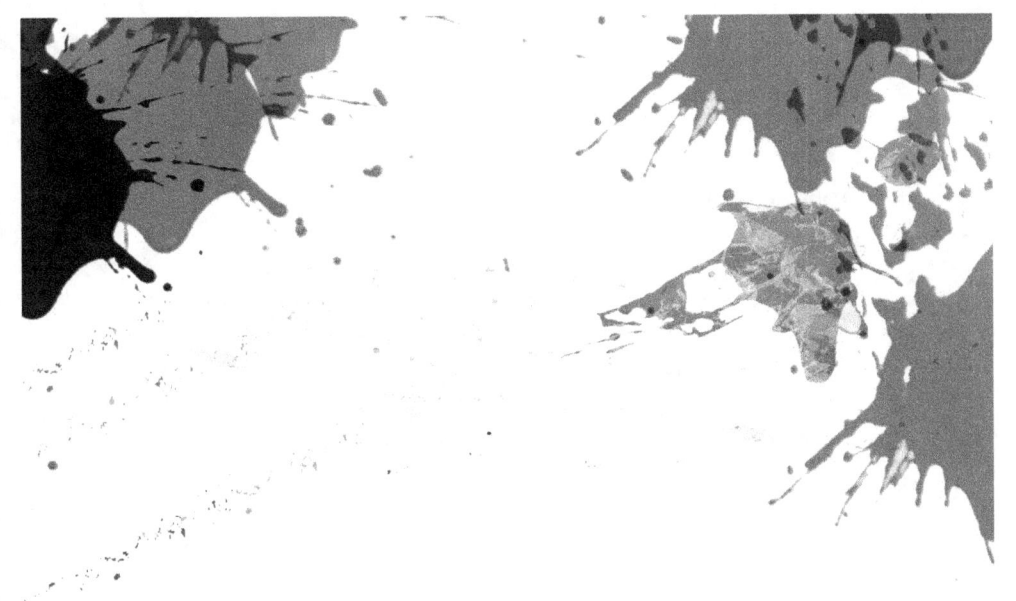

Education

Role of Teacher for Peace Education

Mr. Rajendrakumar Muljibhai Parmar[1]

This paper outlines a framework for developing peace education agenda in high schools and college and university level. Historical peace education programs are reviewed and included into a comprehensive program of substantive, peace education content and pedagogy. The historical programs reviewed include the Integral Model of Peace Education, Learning to stop War, and Master of Arts Program in Peace Education at our school, college & University level for Peace education.

Peace is simply having a feeling of security, calm and restfulness. We often tend to think of peace as being an international issue, far from our daily life, but we do not realize that global peace can only be achieved if each country is established at peace. The peace and happiness of each country can only be achieved if every citizen is at peace. This follows therefore that a country can be peaceful and progress if people live tolerantly. We all want peace of mind. The need of the hour is to develop the young generation with peace consciousness and the importance of conflict resolution. Neither our society nor our educational system has any scope for highlighting the importance of peace and conflict resolution.

In every walk of life our attention is focused on violence, confrontation, competition, self-interest and the need to win. The history of wars is no longer than peace. It took the impact of two world wars and the Hiroshima bomb disaster for human kind to begin to perceive the concept of peace as the primary goal. Our School, college and university teacher can spread massage about the peace in the society through our studying generation. The whole reliant of peace of our nation on the student, simply they can learn and establish in society peace. Here teacher's role is very important to teach student what peace education is and how to maintain in society peace so that, every citizen can be avoid any kind of conflict from neighbor to neighbor country.

[1]Assistant Professor, Shree J M Patel Institute of Social Work and Applied Arts, APMS Campus In Front of Near New Bus Stand, Anand, Gujarat, India

Healthy Practices in Teaching & Learning with Information Technology, and Evaluation Method in Classroom

Mr. Rajendra M Parmar[1], Dr. S. M. Makvana[2]

Thousands of candles can be light from a single candle, and the life of candle will not be reduced. Happiness never decreases by being sharing. One of the most satisfying aspects of teaching at the college or university level may be found in the mentoring connection that faculty members can develop with their students. A good mentoring connection can be what is sometimes called a "peak experience" for both mentor and student. A sharing of something unique that no one else may experience in quite the same way. The student experiences an acceptance of ideas and contributions that may be unequalled in previous life experience.

Although there has been a strong move forward to get educational technology into the hands of teachers and students, many barriers to implementation still exist.

The integration of technology into the curriculum will not succeed without giving teachers sufficient time to practice, explore, conceptualize, and collaborate.

Professional development activities may not provide ongoing, hands-on training for teachers or practical strategies for implementing technology into lesson plans. Initial technology funding may not be sustained and thus not capable of providing upgrades, maintenance, and ongoing professional development. Fortunately, these obstacles can be addressed and overcome. This Critical Issue provides practical information for promoting technology use in schools, college, and university.

[1]Assistant Professor, Shree J M Patel Institute of Social Work and Applied Arts, APMS Campus In Front of Near New Bus Stand, Anand, Gujarat, India
[2]Professor,Department of Psychology,   Sardar Patel University, Vallabh vidyanagar, Gujarat

The Development of Distributive Justice: Does Type of Schooling Really Matter?

Dr. Rita Karmakar[1], Prof. Anjali Ghosh[2]

Ddistributive justice is the normative principle designed to guide the allocation of resources among the members of a community. Distributive justice in the context of reward allocation mainly deals with various determinants of preference for specific justice (allocation) rules, such as equity (merit), equality, need and seniority (Deutsch, 1985; Homans, 1961; Leventhal, 1980). The present study has been undertaken to determine the role of age, gender and type of schooling on the development of distributive justice of children. Participants of the study were 200 children (100 from missionary and 100 from non-missionary schools) belonging to Kolkata district, West Bengal. The results indicated the role of type of schooling and age on the development of distributive justice of adolescents. Pre adolescents generally prefer equality as justice criteria whereas adolescents generally prefer merit as their justice criteria. Effect of type of schooling is prominent among pre-adolescents.

[1]Indian Institute of Management (IIM), Calcutta
[2]Indian Statistical Institute, Calcutta

Academic Achievement of College Students and Their Locus of Control

Ruhanshi Mathur[1]

The main aim of the study was to find out whether the locus of control of the individuals, of college going age, has any effect on their academic performances or not. The objective was to conduct a comparative study of the academic achievement and locus of control of college students. The researcher tried to gather a fair response from the total of 60 subjects between the age group of 18-21. The subjects were chosen randomly within the Pandit Deendayal Petroleum University. This study did not include effect of gender on the responses, as the locus of control is more of a cognitive drive which is independent from the gender specific ideology of the subjects. The research instruments used were Locus of control inventory (which reflects the way in which students feel about what happens in their academic institutions) and Life experience inventory (which reflects the experiences of life). The subjects were made to fill both the questionnaires and then the items were scored and results were analyzed. The scores were given to the subjects' response based on the norms provided. Thereby each questionnaire response was scored and subjects were divided into two groups, namely, High on Internality (I) and Low on Internality (E). Further to this, the subjects were made to supply their overall academic performance grade, which was further analysed for each of the two groups. The two groups showed a clear indication that the group with high internality had a better Mean of their overall performance grade,7.40, whereas the latter showed a weak overall performance grade of 5.93. Also, the two groups showed a well correlation of the type of locus of control as per the locus of control inventory and life experience inventory (0.97), depicting a true locus of control that the subjects follow as per their experiences of life and the way they perceive about their academia in the college. The Mean and Standard deviation of the scores of the two groups were 30,19 and 5,6 respectively. Whereas the Life experience inventory showed a Mean of 17 and 10.

Recommendations: Increase the sample size as that proved to be a limitation to this study. Further more tests could prove a better result for a larger sample size.

A study across ages and socio-economic group is also possible and might give different results.

[1]Student, Pandit Deendayal Petroleum University, Ahmedabad, Gujarat

University Entrance Exam Result and Preparatory Class Average Score as Predictors of College Performance

Yoseph Shumi Robi[1]

The purpose of this study was to assess the degree to which university entrance exam result (UEER) and preparatory class average score (PCAS) predict success in college academic performance. The subjects of this study were 484 students. The data were collected from the Registrar Office. Correlation and regression analyses were employed on the data. The results indicated that PCAS and UEER in order as selection instruments appeared to be valid predictors of first year college CGPA and jointly accounted for 33.70 percent of the variation in college performance. Besides, PCAS was found out to be more important than UEER as admission variable. Based on the findings recommendations were forwarded.

[1]Assistant Professor, Department of Education and Psychology, Kotebe University College, Addis Ababa, Ethiopia

A Study of Academic Anxiety of Secondary School Students With Relation To Their Gender and Religion

Dr. Arvindgiri K. Aparnath[1]

The present study is based on Academic anxiety. The aim of the study is to find out the difference between religion and gender, regarding academic anxiety for the purpose of the study, 120 School children were chosen from different school at Kapadwanj town, Gujarat, for data collection in all 120 student, 60 being boys (30 Hindu +30 Muslim) and 60 girls (30 Hindu + 30 Muslim)

Generally anxiety can be either a trait anxiety or a state anxiety. A trait anxiety is a stable characteristic or trait of the person. A state anxiety is one which is aroused by some temporary condition of the environment such as examination, accident, punishment, etc. Academic anxiety is a kind of state anxiety which relates to the impending danger from the environments of the academic institution including teacher, certain subjects like Mathematics, English, etc. I have used „Academic Anxiety Scale for children" (AASC Scale) by Dr. A. k. Singh & Dr. (km) A. Sen Gupta. The obtained data analyzed through Mann-Whitney „ U „ test. The result shows that there was no significant difference between the Academic anxiety of Muslim boys & girls and Hindu girls & Muslim girls. There is more Academic anxiety in Hindu girls then Hindu boys and more Academic anxiety in Muslim boys then Hindu boys.

[1]Adhyapak sahayak, Department of Psychology, Shah K .S. Arts & V.M. Parekh Commerce College, KAPADWANJ, Dis. Kheda, Gujarat.

A Comparative Study on Dimensions of Role Efficacy between Top and Middle Management of Universities in Rajasthan

Chaudhary A.K[1], Jain N[2]

Role Efficacy showed higher Organizational effectiveness. This depicts that with higher role efficacy in the organization, the employees were more effectively. The purpose of the present research work is to compare role efficacy of top and middle management employees of universities of Rajasthan. Respondents were directly contacted for filling up the standard questionnaire of Role Efficacy Scale, developed by Dr. Udai Pareek. The ten dimensions of role efficacy namely (Centrality, Self-role integration, Proactivity, Creativity, Inter-role linkage, Helping relationship, Superordination, Influence, Personal growth and Coordination) were analysed through t-test. The results conclude that there is significant differences on dimension (self role integration, creativity and inter role linkage) of role efficacy of top and middle management. The significance of the study is based on the challenges facing higher education and to improve their academic standard through role efficacy of top and middle level management.

[1] Dr. Ajay K. Chaudhary, Senior Lecturer, Department of Psychology, Government Meera Girls College, Udaipur (Raj.)
[2] Ms. Namrata Jain, Research Scholar, Faculty of Management, Pacific University, Udaipur.

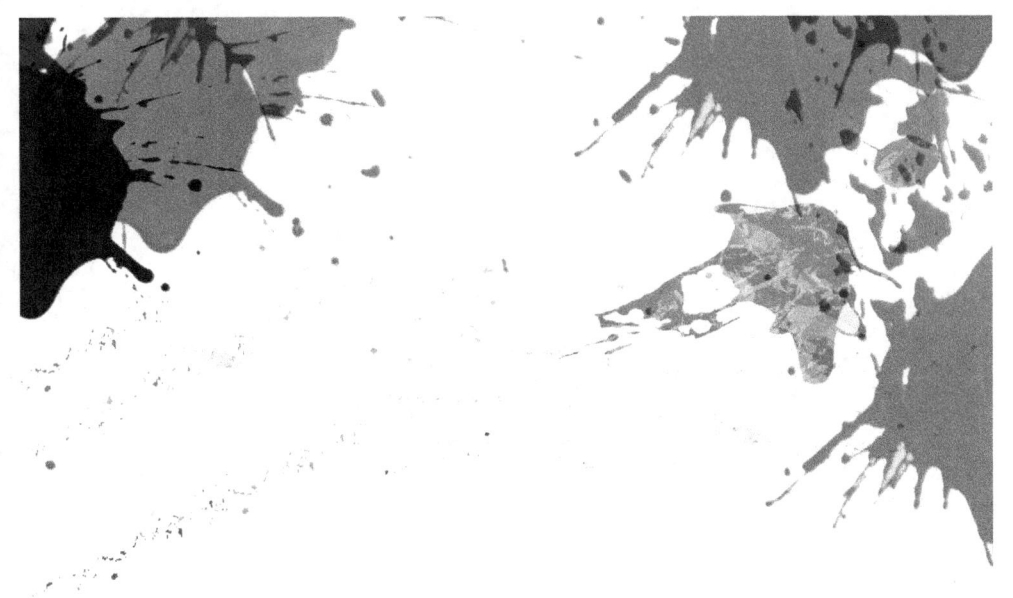

Emotion

Emotional Competence of Adolescents in Joint Family and Nuclear Family

Ms. Hiral Y. Suthar[1]

The present investigation was undertaken to find the impact of emotional competence of adolescents of joint and nuclear family from urban and rural area. The emotional competence scale was administered on 80 adolescents of Vadodara district. Scale was use for data collection is personal datasheet and Emotional competence scale developed by Dr. Sharma H.C and Dr. Bhardwaj R.L (2007). Data were analysis by 't' test. Result show, There is difference found on Emotional competence among adolescent's joint and nuclear family. There is no significant difference in emotional competence of boys and girls. There is no significant difference in emotional competence adolescents of urban and rural area. Adolescents of joint family have better Emotional competence than adolescents of nuclear family. Girls have better emotional competence than boys.

[1]PhD Scholar, Department of Psychology, S P University, Anand , Gujarat

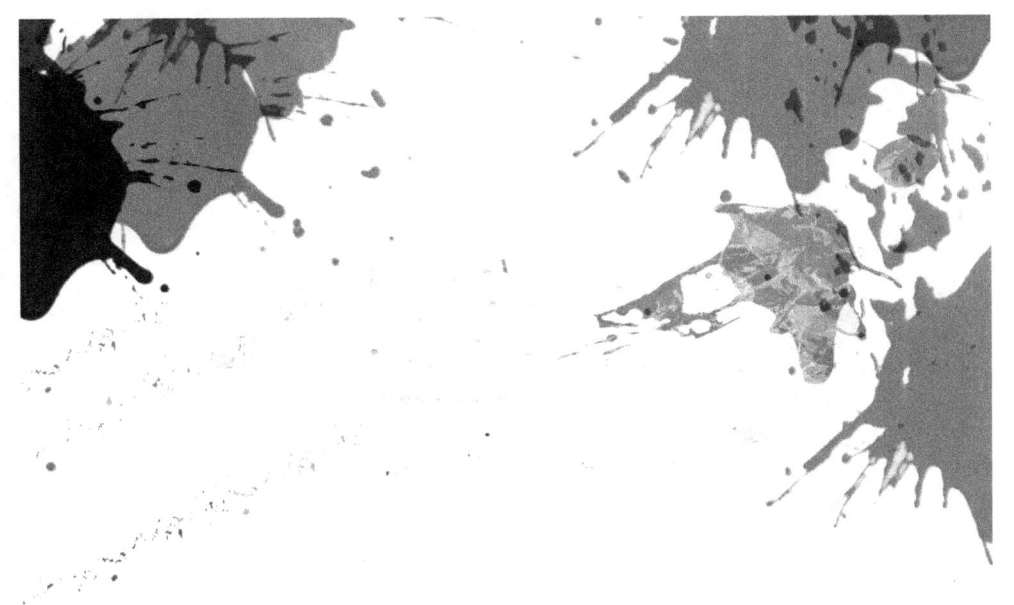

Emotional
Intelligence

Emotional Intelligence among Professors of Granted and Non-Granted Collages: A Comparative Study

Mr. Bhavesh G. Gopani[1]

The aim of present study was to investigate emotional intelligence among professors of granted and non-granted collages. The Random sampling method was used in this study. The total sample consisted 60 professors among this 30 of granted and 30 non-granted collages. Along with the respective personal data sheet and emotional intelligence scale developed by Hayd, Path and Dhar (2001) and it is also translated in Guajarati by Rathod used from data collection. Data was analyzed by „t‟test verify the hypothesis. The result shows that „t‟ value is 4.13 that is significant at 0.01 level. So, the hypothesis is not accepted. It means professor of granted and non-granted was very far difference between emotional intelligence.

[1]M.A, Department of Psychology, Maharaja Krishnakumarshinhji,Bhavnagar University, Bhavnagar, Gujarat.

Emotional Intelligence as a Related To Difference Areas, Stream' and Sex' among School Student

Dr. S. M. Makvana[1]

This is the study was conducted as Emotional intelligence in the variables associated as a Types of area's (rural and urban), types of a streams (Arts and Science), and types of sex as a male and female. On a sample of 240 cases selected from secondary and higher secondary schools student's of Bharuch district of Gujarat state by rendering 2 x 2 x 2 three-factor factorial research design.

The emotional intelligence scale constructed and standardize by Patel and Patel 1985 was used to measured emotional intelligence.

The results reveal that's rural student are more emotional intelligence than urban school students are. In addition, emotional intelligence has be found to the greater in student of science stream compare to arts student and female student's as compare to a student of arts stream and male student's respectively.

[1] Professor, Department of Psychology, Sardar Patel University, Vallabhvidyanagar, GUJARAT-388120

Emotional Intelligence of Boys and Girls Studying In Undergraduate Courses

Maniya Anil A.[1] Chauhan Ajay J.[2]

The present study about of emotional Intelligence Level of Arts and Commerce Students. Total 40 students were selected randomly Anand district area's colleges. In which 20 students (10 males and 10 females) from Arts faculties and also 20 students (10 male and 10 females) from commerce faculty. After analysis was done according to key for the comparison of difference group 't' test was calculated.

[1&2]M.A, Department of psychology, S.P. University, Vallabh Vidyanagar

Self Compassion and Emotional Intelligence of Engineering and Dental College Students

Dr. Thiyam Kiran Singh[1], Ms. Niharika Saini[2]

Total samples of 60 were collected out of which 15 boys and 15 girls were engineering students and the remaining 15 boys and 15 girls were dental students. They were collected using simple random method from different departments of engineering of Amity University Rajasthan (AUR) and Jaipur dental college to compare self compassion & emotional intelligence between Engineering and Dental college students using emotional intelligence scale and self compassion scale. The result found no difference in self compassion of Engineering and Dental students but there is difference in traits of emotional intelligence of boys of Engineering and Dental student. Again the result also found significant difference in overall comparison of Engineering and Dental students in the area of emotional intelligence which proclaim that Engineering students are better in emotional intelligence than Dental students.

[1]Assistant Professor and Clinical Psychologist, Dept. of Psychology, AIBAS, Amity University Rajasthan, Jaipur, Rajasthan
[2]M. Phil Student, Clinical Psychology Trainee at Dept. of Psychology, AIBAS, Amity University Rajasthan, Jaipur, Rajasthan

Gender and Emotional Intelligence of Collage going students

Pooja Verma[1], Dr. Pubalin Dash[2]

Emotional intelligence is social and acquisitive in nature so either consciously or unconsciously parents and children represent their emotion in an expressive way to one another, in their interaction. It seems that further to individual differences of boy and girl, the expectation of society and people around, especially parents, are different in terms of children's sexuality. As per our society, girls are mostly expected to be more expressive of feelings, whereas abstaining from feelings expression in boys is strengthened as a manly model. The research showed that emotional intelligence is meaningful associated with gender differences. The present study examined the effect of effects of emotional intelligence on male and female students. The total participant of the present study is 150 (75 male and 75 female. All students belongs to master level studying in various colleges in Ghaziabad were selected in randomly the data was collected through standardized "Emotional Intelligence Test" by Hydes & Dethe. T-test was conducted to compare between means. Then, an over view of the paper is include a demonstration of the influence of gender differences on Emotional Intelligence is also given. Finally in conclusion it is important to realize that girls are higher than boys in emotional intelligence.

[1]&[2]Indian Institute of Psychology (IIP), Noida, Uttarpradesh

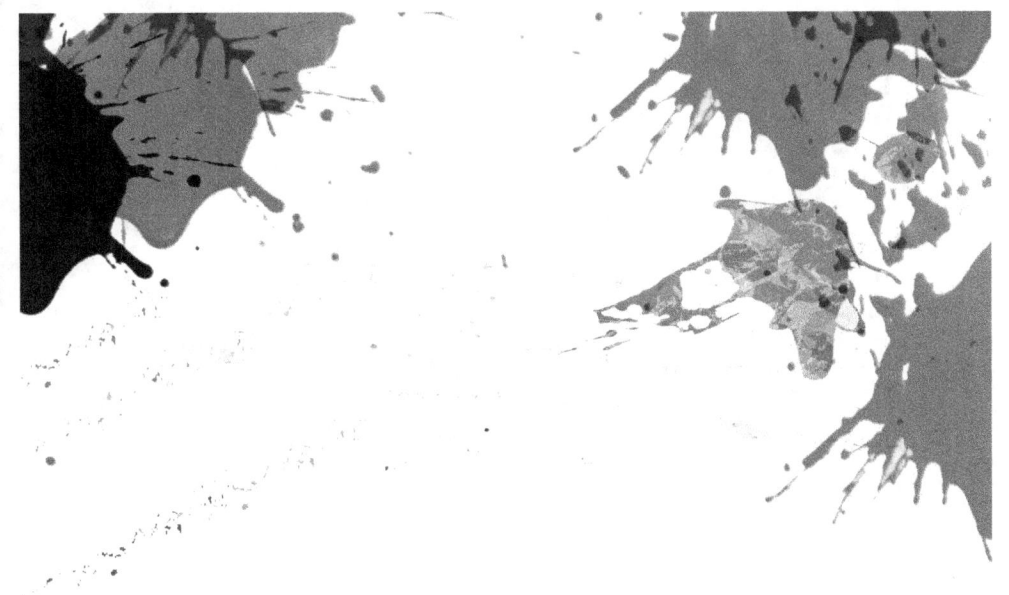

General Issues

T. V. serial and Aggression

Mr. Pravin A Baviskar[1], Dr. N. D. Mundada[2]

The present study was conducted to see the effect of violent t.v.serial on aggression level among the secondary school going students of Jalgaon city. Buss and Perrys Aggression Questionnaire was used to measure the aggression level of the adolescent. For this study a sample of 140 students of age range 14-16 years studying in 9th and 10th classes were selected from different school of Jalgaon city.

[1]Research Fellow, Dept of Psychology, S. S. M. M. College Pachora, Dist Jalgaon. (MS)
[2]Ph.D.Guide, Dept of Psychology, S. S. M. M. College, Pachora, Dist Jalgaon. (MS)

Adolescence at Risk: An Overview

Shaik Ali[1]

Today, 1.2 billion adolescents stand at the crossroads between childhood and the adult world. Around 243 million of them live in India. About one-quarter of India's population are adolescents.(UNICEF). As they stand at these crossroads, so do societies at large – the crossroads between losing out on the potential of a generation or nurturing them to transform society. Adolescence is considered as a period of transition from childhood to adulthood. It is characterized by rapid physical growth, significant physical, emotional, psychological and spiritual changes. Adolescents – young people between the ages of 10 and 19 years are often thought of as a healthy group. Nevertheless, many adolescents do die prematurely due to accidents, suicide, violence, pregnancy related complications and other illnesses that are either preventable or treatable. Many more suffer chronic ill-health and disability. In addition, many serious diseases in adulthood have their roots in adolescence. For example, tobacco use, sexually transmitted infections including HIV, poor eating and exercise habits, lead to illness or premature death later in life. Like adults, adolescents can experience emotions, thoughts, and behaviors that are distressing, disruptive, and disabling. Because many of these problems are precursors to much more disabling disorders during later life, mental and behavioral problems in childhood and adolescence represent a very high cost to society in both human and financial terms.

The problems of adolescents are multi- dimensional in nature and require holistic approach. This paper aims to reveal the various problems of the adolescence in India. It also makes an attempt to locate the significance of measures from a strategic perspective. The present study is based upon secondary sources.

[1]Lecturer in Sociology, Government Pre-University College, Kavital. Tq: Manvi. Dt:Raichur. Karnataka

The Age Differences in Training of the Holistic Living Life Style

Nilaben M. Borad[1]

In the present ties individuals are suffering from various tensions and frustrations. To avoid this, experts are recommending the Holistic Life Style. This life style suggests living the life wholly or perfectly. That means the individual should lead the life completely, not only physically, but mentally and spiritually also. If proper knowledge is given the individual can easily lead Holistic living. In the present study the attempt is made in this direction. All individuals cannot be same in leading the Holistic life style. There would bind to be some differences due to the age. Thus the problem of the study is "The Age differences in Training of the Holistic Living Life Style" For the sample 50 students 10th std. and the 50 students of college were selected randomly. For giving information about the Holistic Living Life Style the special material was prepared. The nature and the diseases due to lac of Holistic Living was mentioned. Different treatments were also discussed. The questionnaire was prepared for this purpose and was used as a tool for the research. The percentage and the t-test were found out. The result showed that there are differences between high school students and college students.

[1]Associated Professor, Mahila Arts and Commerce College, Veraval. Gujarat

Effect of Media on Children Behaviour: Media Psychological Perspective

Mr. Rajput Kiransinh Natwarsinh[1]

There is both Negative and positive effect of Media on Children Behaviour. The first issue of the media's effects on children is violence in the media. By far the greatest amount of psychological research on the media has concerned the impact of televised violence and violence contained within video games on children and concluded that exposure to Media and video game violence leads to increased aggression, an effect that has been demonstrated both as a short term consequence and longer-term effect of excessive exposure. Parents commonly express concern over advertising directed at children, perceiving it as a source of conflict with their children who demand advertised products that parents may feel are inappropriate, and also fearing that it may lead them to adopt overly materialistic values. Media play Importance role in child socialization processes and it play role to teach child cultural values and beliefs. Media also play role in Children education and their awareness about Global issues. Parental Mediation play Importance role to Increase Positive effect of media on children and reduce Negative effect of Media on children.

[1]Teaching Assistant, Department of Psychology, Faculty of Education and Psychology, The M.S. University of Baroda, Vadodara

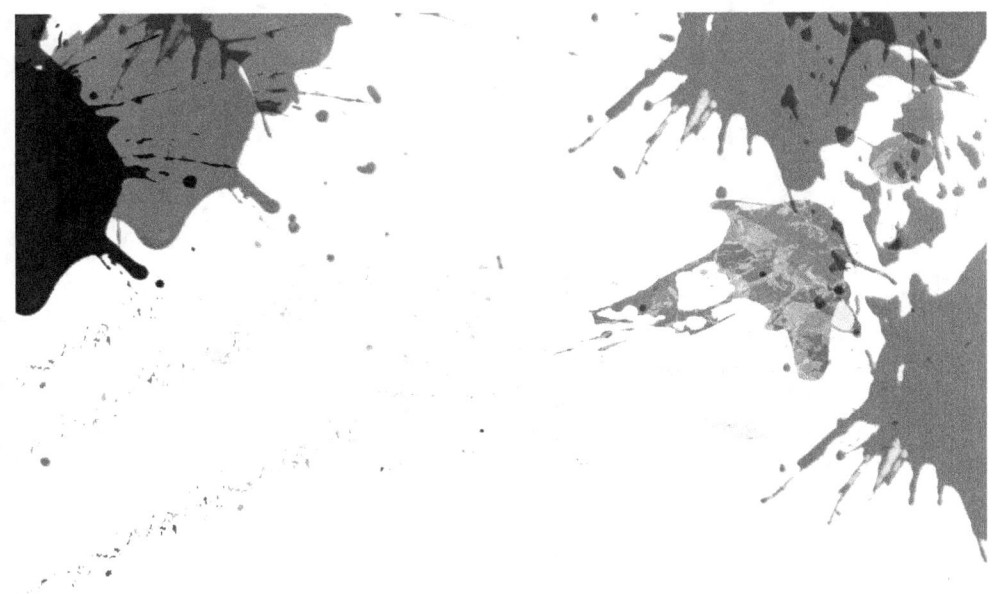

Human
Interaction

The Science of Human Interaction

Shyam Mehta[1]

In the case of a man and woman, there are four forces that drive them together. These four are weak, semi strong, strong or super strong, depending on distance. Distance here is not centimetres or kilometres, but is measured in terms of love and affection. Affection can be negative, which means that you dislike somebody, it can be zero which means that you are indifferent to him or her (for example, you might not know him or her), it can be modest and it can be large. When your affection for your spouse exceeds your affection for yourself, it turns into love. So, this is the measure of distance between a man and a woman.

[1]Student, University of Cambridge, London, United Kingdom

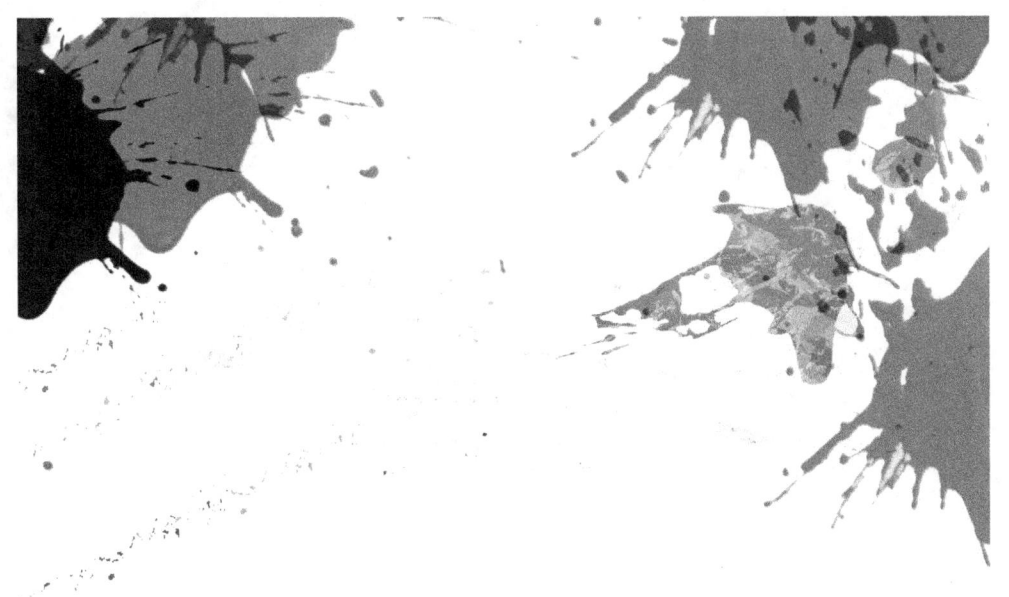

Insecurity

Peer-Group Context Insecurity' in Upper and Lower Class Youth

Mr. Sandipkumar N. Patel[1]

Present study represents a comparative account of Insecurity" in upper and lower class youth. Here we have chosen 18 to 35 years old fellows in both upper and lower class category. Insecurity measurement was carried out by using „Scale of Insecurity" created by Dr. Beena Shah. After statistical analysis of all data, we found vast different in degree of Insecurity between Upper and lower class youth. We have studied School context Insecurity by taking three independent variables using F-Anova test with 2x2x2 factorial design.

[1]Research Scholar, Department of psychology, Sardar Patel University, Vallabh Vidyanagar, Gujarat

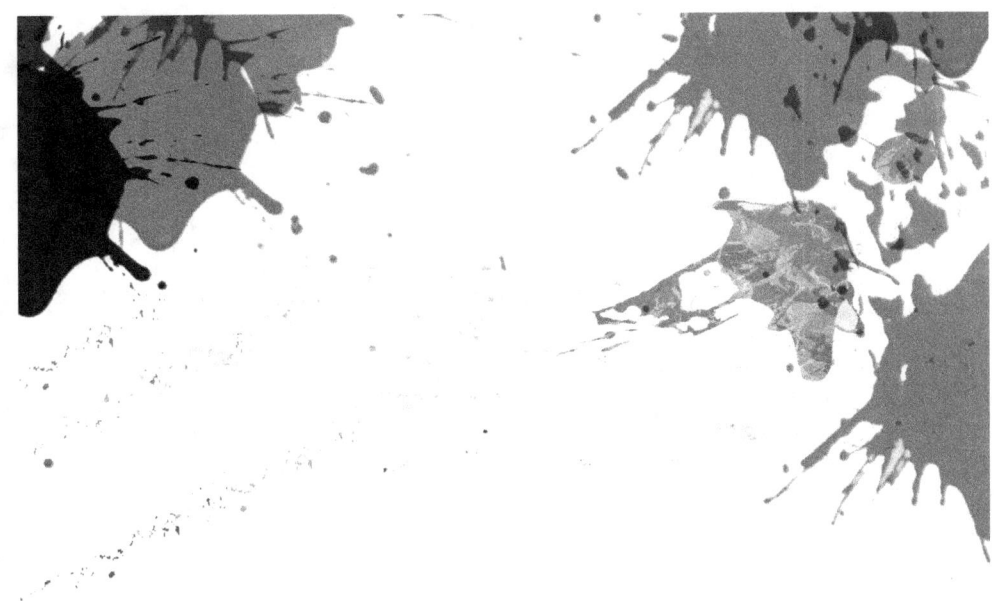

Leadership

Leadership Style of Pharmaceutical and Engineering Company Employees

Jashvantbhai Devda[1], Dr. S. M. Makwana[2]

Aim of the research is to find out the "leadership style among pharmaceutical and engineering company employees" to study by researcher selected three variables one is type of organization, second is category was employee and third of education qualification. The groups have 300 employs. In each group has 150 pharmaceutical employees and other one groups has 150 engineering employees. Scale was use for data collection is personal datasheet and leadership style scale developed by L. I. Bhushan (2005), 2x2x3 factorial design was used and data were analysis by „F" test. Result show, there was significant difference of leadership style between pharmaceutical and engineering company employees, the leadership style scores of engineering company employee is higher than pharmaceutical company employee. There was significant difference of the leadership style between manager and worker of pharmaceutical and engineering company employees, the leadership style scores of manager is higher than worker. There was no significant difference of the leadership style between post-graduate, graduate and diploma degree holder of pharmaceutical and engineering company employees. There was no significant interaction effect of the leadership style between types of organization and category of employees of pharmaceutical and engineering company employees. There was no significant interaction effect of the leadership style between types of organization and education qualification of pharmaceutical and engineering company employees.

[1]M.Phil researcher Scholar, Dept. of Psychology, Saradar Patel University, Vallbh vidhyanagar-388120 Gujarat

[2]Professor, Department of Psychology, Sardar Patel University, Vallbh vidhyanagar-388120 Gujarat

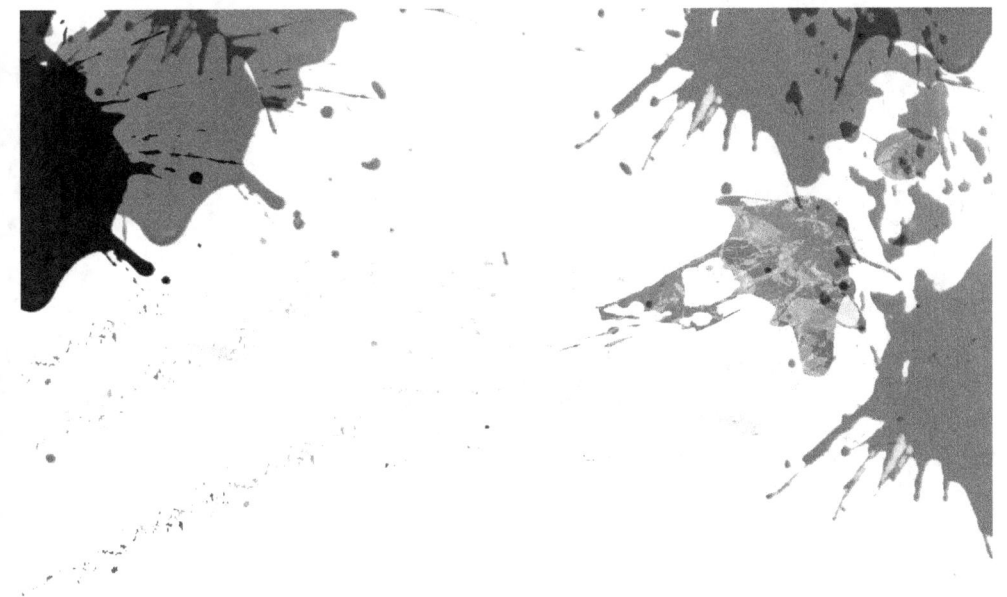

Mental Health

Mental Health among Professor and Primary Women Teacher: A Comparative Study

Kothival Krishna P[1]

The main purpose of this research was to find out the mean difference between professor and primary teacher women in mental health. The total sample consisted 60 women were taken. The research tool for mental health was measured by Dr. Jagdish and Dr. A. K. Srivastava. Here 't' test was applied to check the significance of mental health in professor and primary teacher. Result shows that No Significant difference between professor and primary teacher in mental health.

[1]Department of psychology, Maharaja Krishnakumarsinhji, Bhavnagar University, Bhavnagar

Mental Health among Joint and Separate Family's Women: A Comparative Study

Ahir Archana P[1]

The main purpose of this research was to find out the mean difference between joint family and separate family's women in mental health. The total sample consisted 60 women were taken. The research tool for mental health was measured by Dr. Jagdish and Dr. A. K. Srivastava. Here 't' test was applied to check the significance of mental health in joint and separate family's women. Result shows that significant difference between joint and separate family's women in mental health.

[1]Department of psychology, Maharaja Krishnkumarshinji, Bhavnagar University

Mental Health for Lady Teachers of Government and Private Schools

Rathod Chirag R[1], Patel Priyanka D[2]

The present study related to mental health level of government and private school's lady, teachers. Total 40 teachers were selected randomly from Bhavnagar district area's School. In which 20 teacher's (10 teacher's 21 to 30 and 10 teacher's 1 to 40 year) from government school's teachers and also 20 teachers (10 teacher's 21 to 30 and 10 teacher's 31 to 40 year.) From private school teachers. After data analysis done with 't' test.

[1&2] M.A, Department of Psychology, S.P. University, VallabhVidyanagar

Mental Health among Married and Unmarried Women

Alpesh B. Kotar[1]

The main purpose of this research was to find out the main difference between married and unmarried women's mental health. The total sample consists of 60 women (30 married and 30 unmarried women). Sample was taken from Bhavnagar city. Scale was use for data collection is mental health scale by Dr. A. K. Shreevastav and Dr. Jagdish (1983). Data was analyzed by 't' test. Result show, there is significant difference between the married and unmarried women.

[1]Assistant Professor, Department of Psychology, Nandkunvarba Mahila Arts College, Bhavnagar

Mental Health of Working and Non Working Women in Ahmadabad

Kiranben Vaghela[1]

Present researches have been done to know the effect of Working and Non Working Women"s mental health. For this Total number of sample was 60 in which 30 working women from the age group of 20 to 40 years; And 30 non working women were taken the same age group. For the data collection MHI (Mental Health Inventory) by Dr. A. K Shriwastav was used for data analysis and concluded result,,t" test was used. For this dimension implies that in positive sense that there is significant difference between working and non working women. The result indicate that working women a lot differ on mental health score as compared to non working women, working women have shown better mental health in compared to non working women .

[1]PhD Scholar, Department of Psychology, Sardar Patel University, Vallabh Vidhya Nagar Anand

Mental Health and Marital Adjustment among Working and Non Working Women

Sonalba G. Parmar[1]

The study was conducted to assess the status of mental health and marital adjustment of the working and non working women. The random sample consisted of 30 working women and 30 non working women selected. Mental Health Inventory by Dr. A.K. Shreevastav and Dr. Jagdish and marital adjustment inventory by P. Kumar and K. Rohatgi. Here t' test was applied to check the significance of mental health and marital adjustment in working and non working women.

The result shows that there is a significant difference between working and non working women in mental health and marital adjustment so the Hypothesis is not accepted.

[1]Assistant Professor, Nandkunvarba Mahila College, Maharaja Krishnakumarsihnji Bhavnagar University. Gujarat

Sports for Positive Mental Health: A Comparative Study of Mental Health among Individual Athletes, Team Athletes and Non-Athletes

Dr. Milan P. Patel[1], Mr. Ankur D. Chaudhari[2]

Mental Health affects our ability to make the most of the opportunities that come our way and play a full part amongst our family, workplace, community and friends. It"s also closely linked with our physical health. Whether we call it well-being, emotional welfare or mental health, it"s key to living a fulfilling life.

The purpose of the study was to compare the Mental Health status among Individual Athletes, Team Athletes and Non-Athletes. Purposive sampling was done in which subjects for the present study were 148 male students of Navsari Agricultural University, Navsari studying various courses in the academic year 2013-14. The Mental Health Scale prepared by Dr .D .J.Bhatt and Ms. Geeta R. Geedawas used as a tool for the present study.

The scores arrived from 45 Individual Athletes, 51 Team Athletes and 52 Non-Athletes were compared by applying the „F" test. The resultant value 7.566 was found significant at the predetermined confidence level of 0.5. Further, this study revealed significant difference between the mean score of Team Athlete & Non-Athlete, whereas there was no significant difference between the Individual Athlete & Team

Athlete and that of Individual Athlete & Non-Athlete. Thus it was evident that Mental Health of Team Athlete was significantly better in comparison to Individual Athlete and Non-Athlete. This clearly shows that those who participate in team games have more chances to stay mentally fit as they involve themselves in preparing mentally for various team competitions. Mental Health is considered to be one of the important components of daily life style. This is certainly an important factor for all of us to live better and longer life. Thus, we all should daily participate in physical activity to stay physically and mentally fit.

[1]Physical Instructor, College of Veterinary Science and A.H., Navsari Agricultural University, Navsari, Gujarat
[2]Physical Instructor, N.M. College of Agriculture, Navsari Agricultural University, Navsari, Gujarat

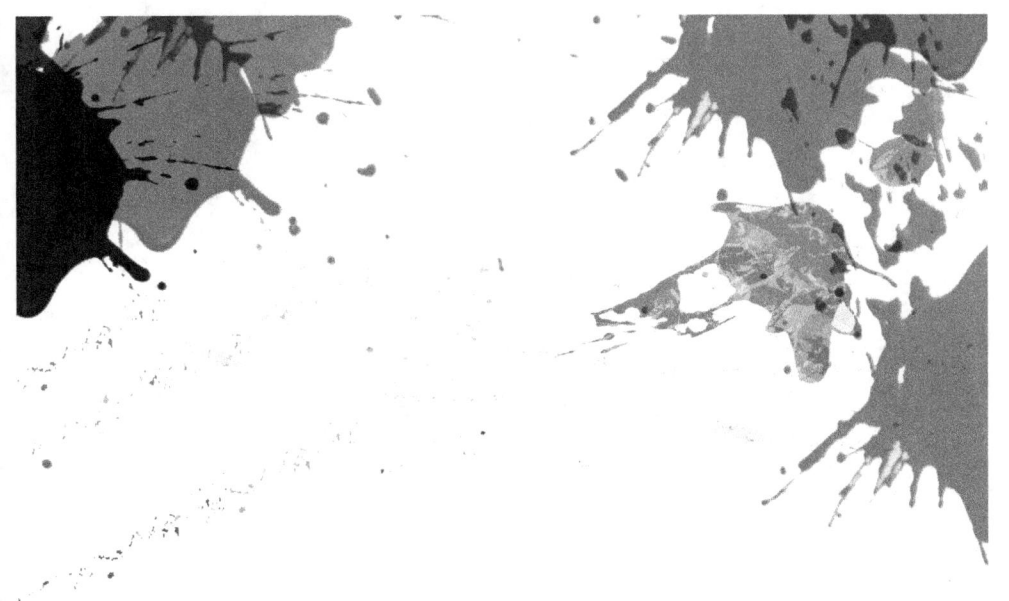

Personality

Ectomorphic and Endomorphic Personality: A Study of Emotional Quotient among Women

Urvashi Sharma[1], Dr. Ravindra Kumar[2]

The main objective of the present study is to examine the Emotional Quotient (sensitivity, conscientiousness, empathy and adaptability) among ectomorphic and endomorphic personality women. A sample of 30 participants (15 ectomorphy personality & 15 Endomorphic personality types) was drawn randomly from the population. Emotional quotient scale by Prof. N. K. Chadha was used for data collection. Data was collected by a face to face interview method. Mean, standard deviation and 't' test were the statistics calculated. The results indicate that there is no significant difference between ectomorphic and endomorphic women in relation to sensitivity, conscientiousness, empathy and adaptability. Results revealed that ectomorphic women have higher sensitivity, empathy and adaptability. On the other hand, the endomorphic women have higher conscientiousness.

[1]Student, PGDGCP, Indian Institute of Psychology, Noida (U.P.) INDIA

[2]Assistant Professor, Department of Psychology, Mewar University, Chittorgarh (Rajasthan)

Correlation between Personality Types and Colour Shade Preference

Divya Ghorawat[1], Ravina Madan[2]

The main aim of this study was to find out whether the color shade preferences of individuals, grouped according to their personality types are alike or not. The researchers also tried to study the difference in color shade preferences based on gender differences. The objective was to understand whether the color shade preferences of individuals are affected by their individual personality types or not and whether gender plays any role in selection of color shades of individuals. The study sample consisted of a total of 80 subjects, randomly selected from within the age group of 18-25. An attempt was made to maintain a balance between two genders and across the ages. The research instruments used were Eysenck's Personality Test (to measure the personality types) and a separate Colour Bar- Colour Preference Test was designed to serve the purpose of this study. The subjects were made to fill both the questionnaires and then the items were scored and results were analyzed. Positive scoring was done for Eysenck's personality questionnaire and negative scoring was used to score the Colour Bar-Colour Preference Test. The data collected was divided into: Introverts (female, male) and Extroverts (female, male). From the data collected the mean, standard deviation and correlation between extraversion scores and the most preferred colour scores, for all the four groups. The mean, standard deviation, and correlation for the four groups was found to be 436.4 (IF), 529.2 (IM), 504 (EF),

453.4 (EM); 5.47 (IF), 6.52 (IM), 5.48 (EF), 6.93(EM); -0.3 (IF), -0.1 (IM), 0.1 (EF) and 0.5 (EM) respectively. From this the conclusion was drawn that there was no significant correlation found between the personality types and colour shade preferences of the subjects except in the case of extroverted males. Recommendations: Increase the sample size as that proved to be a limitation to this study.

A study across ages is also possible and might give different results.

[1]&[2] Researcher, Pandit Deendayal Petroleum University. Ahmedabad, Gujarat

Personality and Emotional Maturity of Depressive and Obsessive Compulsive Disorders

Dr. Thiyam Kiran Singh[1], Akanksha Sharma[2]

In this study random sampling technique was used in which a sample of 30 Depressive patients and 30 Obsessive Compulsive Disorder (OCD) patients were collected with the age range of 18 to 40 years. The participants were administered Dimensional Personality Inventory developed by Bhargav (1997) and Emotional Maturity Scale developed by Singh and Bhargave (1991). The purpose of the study is to compare Depressive and OCD patients on Personality Inventory Test and Emotional Maturity Scale to find out any significant difference in overall personality and its various dimensions similarly as well as overall Emotional Maturity and its various dimensions. The result found no significant in overall personality and its dimensions. Likewise, the result also found no significant difference in overall Emotional maturity but there is significant difference under the dimensions of Emotional Progression and Independence which gives the impression that depressive patients are more emotionally progressed or improved but less independent comparing with O.C.D. patients.

[1]M.A., M.Phil (M&SP), Ph.D (Clinical Psychology), Assistant Professor, Dept. of Psychology, AIBAS, Amity University Rajasthan.
[2]M.Phil Clinical Psychology trainees. AIBAS, Amity University Rajasthan.

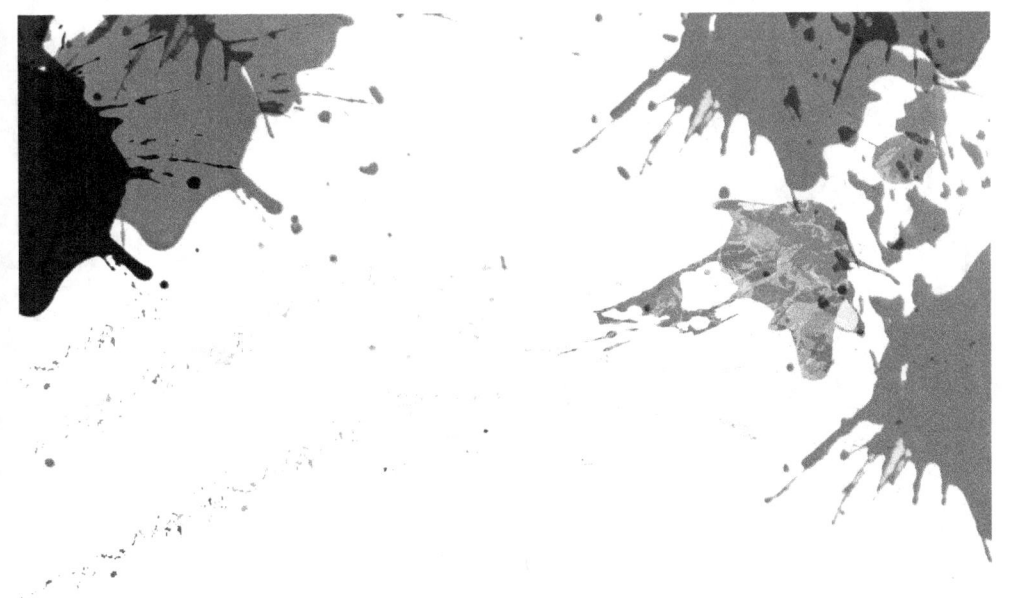

Religious

Five Factor Model in Iranian Culture: A Psychometrics Analysis of NEO-Five Factor Inventory (NEO-FFI)

Manoochehr Azkhosh[1], Ali Asgari[2]

This study aimed to investigate the construct validity and factor structure of NEO-Five Factor Inventory (Costa & McCrae, 1992) in Iranian population. Participants were 1639 (780 male, 859 female) Tehran people aged 15-71. The results of explanatory factor analysis showed no notable differences between the factor structures extracted by oblique and orthogonal rotations and didn"t replicate the scoring key. The Openness and Agreeableness had more psychometric problems (low internal consistency and high deleted items). The female"s NEO-FFI factor structure (with 41 items of60 loaded on intended factors)was clearer than males" (with 37 items). Confirmatory factor analysis supported the male"s latent modeling of the 31-item but failed to fit the female"s model. The women scored significantly higher in the Neuroticism, Openness, Agreeableness, and Conscientiousness than men who scored significantly higher in the Extraversion. As previous findings, the current results showed the NEO-FFI"s cultural limitations assessing the universality of the Five Factor Model.

[1]&[2], Professor, University of Social Welfare and Rehabilitation sciences, Iran

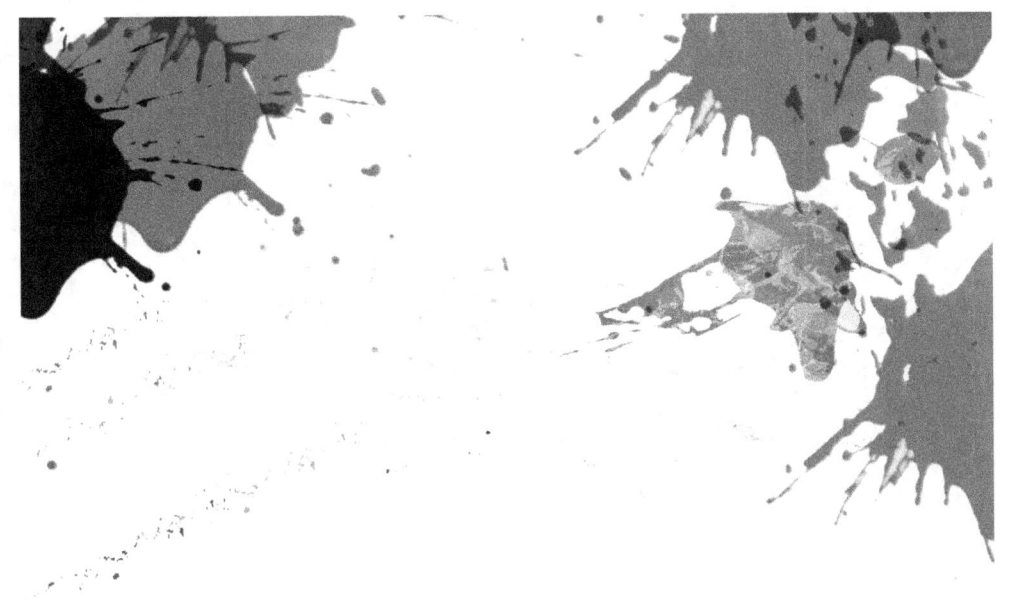

Self Concept

Self Concept of Aids Positive & Negative Tribal and Non Tribal Women

Ankit P. Patel[1]

The presents study was held in area of PANCHMAHAL district. Aim of the study is to measure the difference of AIDS positive & negative tribal and non tribal women, about self concept. 80 women were selected randomly from Godhra' Civil hospital and Local area. In which 20 tribal and 20 non tribal from AIDS positive and tribal and 20 non tribal AIDS negative women. For present study "MENTALHEALTH BATTERY" (MHB) of Arunkumar Singh and Alpna Sen Gupta was used. From this battery only 15 items were selected (related to self concept) for the research. For this comparison's t test was used. Result is that there is a no significant difference in self concept of women.

[1]MA, Dept. of Psychology, SARDAR PATEL University, Vallabh VidhyaNagar

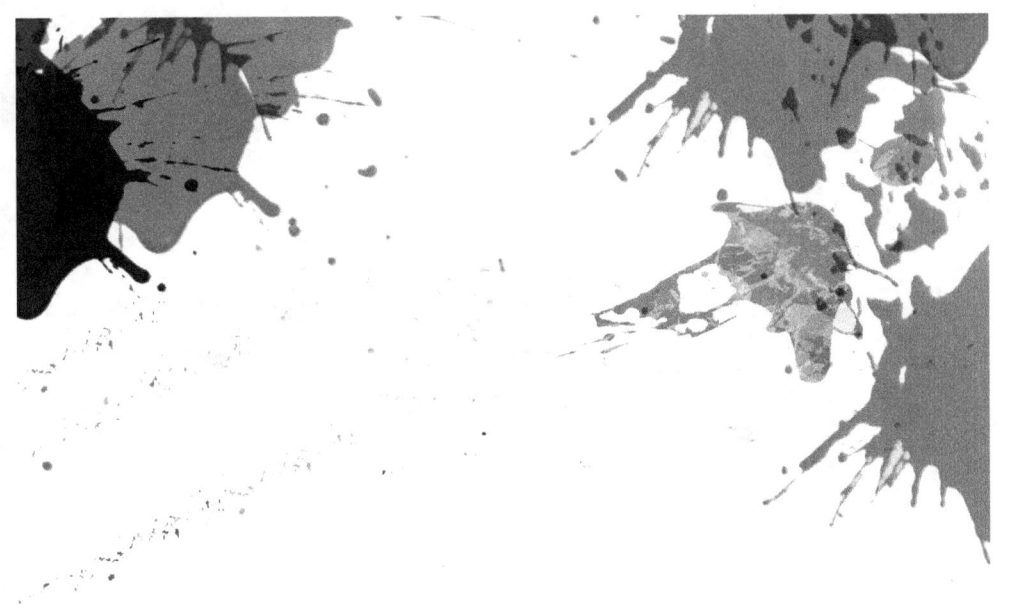

Job Satisfaction

Job Satisfaction and Organizational Commitment among Public and Private Engineers

Deepak Bhardwaj[1], Shilpa Chouhan[2]
Subhash Meena[3]

The present study is aimed at exploring the job satisfaction and organizational commitment among engineers of government and private organizations. Sample of the study consisted of 25 government engineers and 25 private engineers belong to Jodhpur District. All the employees have been in the age range of 30 to 45 years with service experience ranges between 5 to 15 years and may be of both the services and working in government and private sectors. For this purpose Job Descriptive Index (Smith, Kendall and Hulin, 1969) adopted for Indian settings by Sayeed and Sinha (1981) and further translated in Hindi (by the standard two-time process) and successfully used on a sample other than industrial organizations (Sinha, 1993) and Organization commitment scale developed by Puja Gupta, (2003) was used. Results indicated there is significant difference between engineers of government and private organizations on job satisfaction and organizational commitment.

[1]Research Scholar (deepakbhardwaj32@gmail.com),
[2]Research Scholar (shilpachouhan15@gmail.com),
[3]Research Scholar (sbhshmeena@yahoo.com), Department of Psychology, Jai Narain Vyas University, Jodhpur.

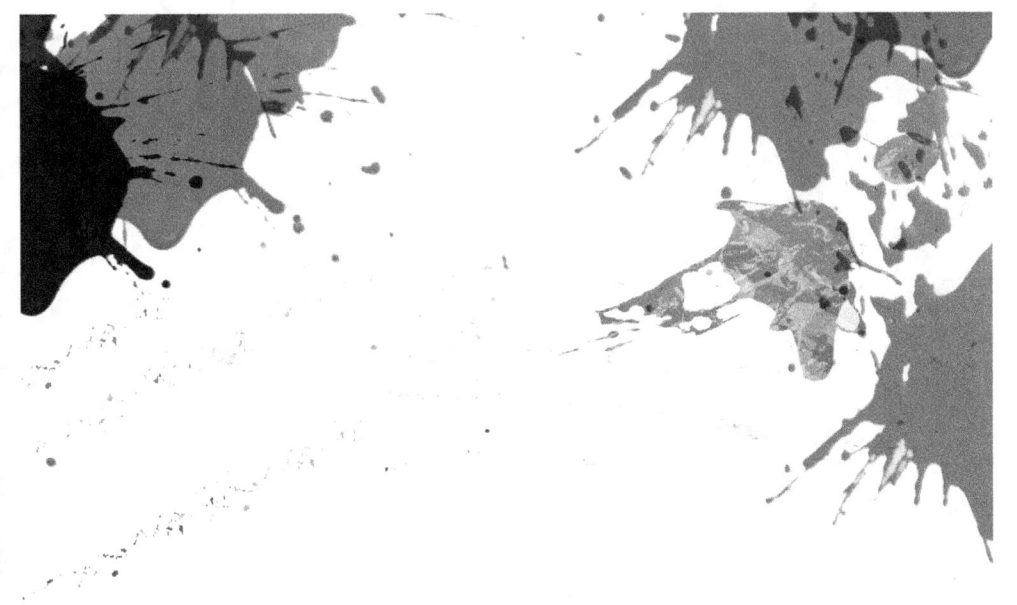

Stress

Stress Management of Old Age

Ankit Patel[1]

In 21st century, problem of old age adjustment is there. Most of the old age persons are suffering from severe stress. How they manage the stress and fell the stress, is disused in this paper. The presents study was held in area of MAHISAGAR district. Aim of the study is to measure the difference of old persons from join family and old age home groups, about stress management level. 100 old persons were selected randomly from MAHISAGAR area. In which 50 old male and female from join family and 50 old male and female from old age home. For present study **"STRESS MANAGEMENT QUESTIONNAIRE (SMQ)"** of Dr. Jim Petersen (1976) was used. After data collection, data was analyzed according to key. t test was calculated for major groups. Main hypothesis was rejected. Causes of rejection are discussed in full length research paper, May more hypotheses are also discussed in paper. Some interactional hypothesis is accepted. This is the interesting area of my research. New suggestions are also mention in full paper. Really this is the current problem of our society. That"s why this research work is important and useful of society.

[1]M.A, Clinical Psychology, SP University, Vallabh Vidyanagar

Stress Management among Teaching & Non - Teaching Staff

Pooja Verma[1], Dr. Ravindra Kumar[2]

The main objective of the present investigation is to examine the stress management among teaching and non teaching staff. A sample of 30 participants (15=Teaching & 15 Non Teaching) was drawn randomly drawn from the population. Stress Management Scale (SMS) by Dr. Pushpraj Singh & Anjali Srivastava was used for data collection. Data was collected by face to face interview method from the target population from different education institute of Ghaziabad city. Mean, standard deviation and t-test were calculated for the analysis of data. Results indicate that there is no significant difference among Teaching and Non-teaching staff participants in relation to stress management. Result revealed that Non teaching participants have higher mean score on stress management in compare to teaching participants. In simple terms it can be said that Non teaching participants have higher stress management.

[1]Student, PGDGCP, Indian Institute of Psychology, Noida (U.P.) INDIA
[2]Assistant Professor, Dept of Psychology, Mewar University, Chittorgarh (Rajasthan)

Depression among B.Ed College Students

Ramesh O. Prajapati[1]

Aim of the research is to find out the depression among B.ed College students, So, investigator selected two groups one is male and other is female, both groups have 120 students. In each group has 60 male and other one groups has 60 female students. Data were collected from different collages of v.v.nagar city. Scale was use for data collection is personal datasheet and depression scale developed by A.T. Back (1967), 2x2 factorial design was used and data were analysis by ANOVA test. Result show, There is significant difference between the depression among male and female B.ed college student. There is significant difference between the depression among urban and rural B.ed college student. There is significant difference between the effect of interaction on depression among type of sex and type of area of B.ed college student.

[1]Ph.D Student, Department of Psychology, S.P.University, V.V.Nagar, Gujarat.

A Study of Academic Stress among Senior Secondary Students

Kartiki Porwal[1], Dr. Ravindra Kumar[2]

The main objective of the present study is to examine the academic stress among senior secondary students. The total participants of the study were 30 (15 male and 15 female). All students belong to 12th standard studying in Noida. The Data was collected through standardized Academic Stress Questionnaire (ASQ) by Akram, Mohd Ilyas Khan and Sahiba Baby. Mean, Standard deviation and T-test were conducted for analysis of data. Result indicates that there is significant difference among boys and girls in relation to academic stress. Result revealed that senior secondary boys have higher academic stress in compare to girls.

[1]M.A Student, Indian Institute of Psychology, Noida, Uttar Pradesh
[2]Assistant Professor, Department of Psychology, Mewar University, Chittorgarh, Rajasthan

Life Satisfaction and Stress Level among Working and Non-Working Women

Dr. Shashi Kala Singh[1]

The main aim of the present study was to examine the life satisfaction and stress among working and non-working women. A sample of 200 women (100working &100non-working) was drawn randomly from the population. Life Satisfaction Scale by Alam & Srivastava (1996) and stress scale by Singh (2004) were used for data collection. Mean, standard deviation, „t‟ test and correlation were the statistics calculated. The results indicated that there was significant difference regarding life satisfaction and stress between working and non-working women. Results revealed that working and non-working women differed significantly on their life satisfaction (t=5.52).Working women were more satisfied with their life, on stress scale non-working women have higher level stress as compared to working women. A significant negative relationship was found between life satisfaction and stress.

[1]Associate Professor, Dept. of Psychology, Ranchi University, Ranchi, Zarkhand

Stress Manage by Yoga

Dr. Jayesh N. Bhalala[1]

Stress management is the need of the hour. However hard we try to go beyond a stress situation, life seems to find new ways of stressing us out and plaguing us with anxiety attacks. There can be innumerable stress factors since different individuals react differently to the same stress conditions. The brain doesn't differentiate between real and imagined stress. Failure in adopting a realistic attitude to events creates symptoms of depression and aggravates stress situations. Do "stressed out" parents necessarily have stressed out kids? Besides being at higher genetic risk for stress, children of stressed parents can also learn the tendency to get stressed out in reaction to life's challenges from their parents."Children of stressed out parents are more likely to be ill equipped to handle stressors positively. Research shows that nicotine dependency actually increases stress levels in smokers-adults and adolescence alike. Adolescent smokers report increasing levels of stress as they develop regular patterns of smoking. The repeated occurrence of stressed moods between smoking means that smokers tend to experience distinctly above-average levels of daily stress. When adults quit smoking, they become less stressed rather than more stressed. Reduces stress hormones (studies shows, laughter induces reduction of at least four of neuroendocrine hormones—epinephrine, cortisol, dopac, and growth hormone, associated with stress response).It is well known that either a quick or constant stress can induce risky mind-body disorders. Stressed out individuals carry a great deal of physical tension in their bodies. Under stress the stiff muscles restrict the circulation of blood. Yogic asanas, meditation and breathing can help stress affected persons in many ways such as:(1)Reduce stress and tension. and (2) Mindfulness meditation helps stress reduction, improving physical and mental health.

[1]Lecturer, Smt. R. R. Patel Mahila College, RAJKOT-360 004,GUJ. INDIA

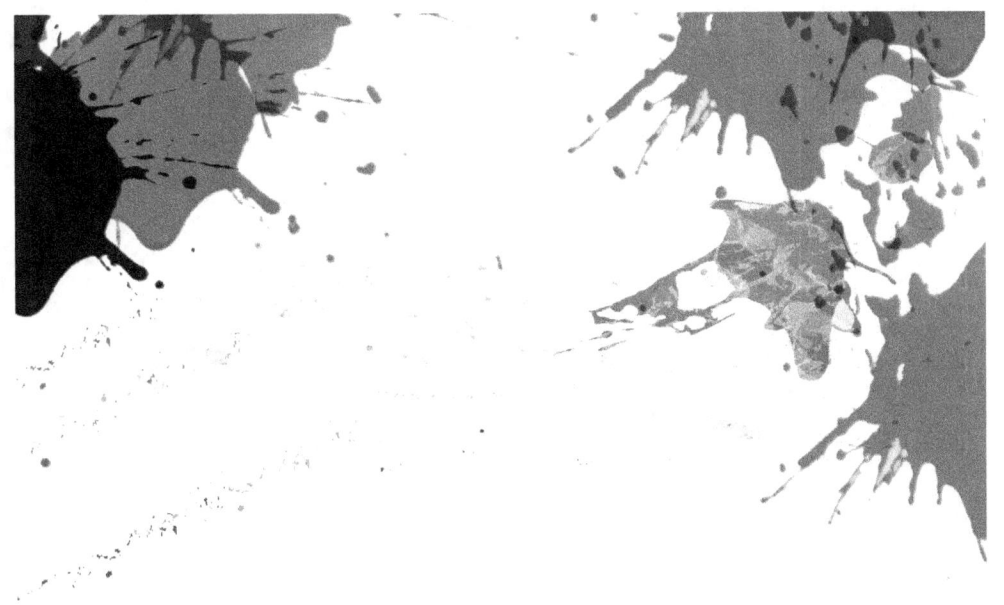

Well-Being

The Psychological Well-Being among Joint and Nuclear Families: A Comparative Study

Ramesh O. Prajapati[1]

Aim of the research is to find out the Psychological Well-being among joint and nuclear families. So investigator selected two groups one is joint families and other is nuclear families, both groups have 200 persons. In one group has 89 and other one groups has 111 persons. The all subjects were randomly selected. Data were collected from Ahmedabad district. Scale was use for data collection is personal datasheet and Psychological Well-being scale developed by Bhogale and Prakash (1995), and data were analysis by „t‟ test. Result show, There is no significant difference between the psychological well-being of joint and nuclear family. There is no significant difference between the psychological well-being of married and unmarried person's.

[1]Department of Psychology, S P University, V.V.Nagar-388 120, Gujarat

Psychological Well Being among B.Ed College Student

Mukesh C. Rathwa[1]

Aim of the research is to find out the psychological Well being among B.ed college students, so investigator selected two groups one is male and other is female, both groups have 120 students. In each group has 60 male and other one groups has 60 female students. Data were collected from different collages of v.v.nagar city. Scale was use for data collection is personal datasheet and psychological Well being scale developed by Bhogale and Prakash (1995), 2x2 factorial design was used and data were analysis by ANOVA test. Result show, There is no significant difference between the Psychological Well being among male and female B.ed college student. There is no significant difference between the Psychological well-being among urban and rural B.ed college student. There is no significant difference between the effect of interaction on Psychological Well being among type of sex and type of area of B.ed college student.

[1]M.Phil Student, Department of Psychology, S.P.University, V.V.Nagar-388 120,, Gujarat

The Psychological Well Being among Hindu and Muslim Educated Unemployed People: A Comparative Study

Sunil S. Jadav[1], Dr. Pankaj S. Suvera[2]

Aim of the research is to find out the Psychological Well being among educated unemployed peoples so investigator selected two groups one is Hindu and other is Muslim educated unemployed people, both groups have 200 peoples. In one group has 135 Hindu and other one groups has 65 Muslim educated unemployed people. The all subjects were randomly selected. Data were collected from Banaskantha district. Scale was use for data collection is personal datasheet and Psychological Well being scale developed by Bhogale and Prakash (1995), and data were analysis by „t‟ test. Result show, There is no significant mean difference between the Psychological well-being of Hindu and Muslim educated unemployed people. There is no significant mean difference between the Psychological well- being of law and middle income families educated unemployed people. There is no significant mean difference between the Psychological well-being of middle and high income families educated unemployed people. There is no significant mean difference between the Psychological well being of law and high income families educated unemployed people. There is no significant mean difference between the Psychological well-being of joint and nuclear families educated unemployed people.

[1]PhD, Research Scholar, Dept. of Psychology, S P University, V.V.Nagar-388 120, Gujarat,
[2] Assistant Professor, Department of Psychology, S P University, V.V.Nagar-388120, Gujarat

Happiness and Wellbeing

Ruchi Sundriyal[1], Dr. Ravindra Kumar[2]

Happiness is a mental or emotional state of well-being characterized by positive or pleasant emotions ranging from contentment to intense joy. Happiness as a concept seems to be readily embraced by the majority of people and appears to be more valued than the pursuit of money, moral goodness or going to heaven. Philosophers and religious thinkers often define happiness in terms of living a good life, or flourishing, rather than simply as an emotion. Happiness economics suggests that measures of public happiness should be used to supplement more traditional economic measures when evaluating the success of public policy. Happy people are healthy people. Happy people live longer and enjoy a greater quality of life. They function at a higher level, utilizing their personal strengths, skills, and abilities to contribute to their own well-being as well as that of others and society. Wellbeing is a contented state of being happy and healthy and prosperous. Psychological well-being refers to how people evaluate their lives. These evaluations may be in the form of cognitions or in the form of affect. The cognitive part is an information based appraisal of one's life that is when a person gives conscious evaluative judgments about one's satisfaction with life as a whole. Most people evaluate their life as either good or bad, so they are normally able to offer judgments. People invariably experience moods and emotions which have a positive effect or a negative effect. We can define psychological well-being in terms of internal experience of the respondent and their own perception of their lives. People have a level of subjective well-being even if they do not often consciously think about it, and the psychological system offers virtually a constant evaluation of what is happening to the person.

[1]Indian Institute of Psychology, NOIDA (U.P.)
[2]Department of Psychology, Mewar University, Chittorgarh (Rajasthan)

Effects of Personal Variables of Call Centre Employees on their Psychological Well Being

Nitin R. Korat[1], Gandharva R. Joshi[2]

The study was designed to investigate the impact of certain personal variables on psychological well being of call centre employees. The sample consisted of 240 call centre employees (120 Male/120 Female) selected randomly from Vodafone Call Centre of Ahmedabad city. Psychological well being scale of Dr. Bhogle and Prakash was used. Results revealed that there exists a significant difference between psychological well being and variables such as Sex, Age, Type of Family, work Shifts and working time of Call center employees. No significant deference observed between Psychological well being of married and unmarried employees. And also no significant difference was found between Psychological well being and Education of Call centre employees.

[1]Research Scholar, **Professor, Department of Psychology, Saurashtra University Rajkot-360005.

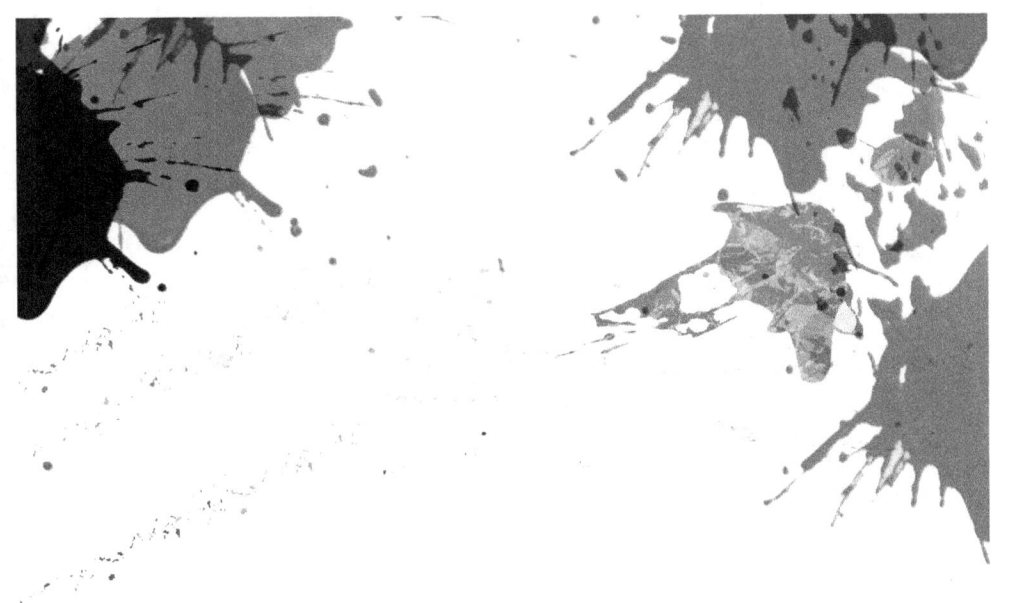

Work Value

Work Value among Married and Unmarried Person': A Comparative Study

Ramesh O. Prajapati[1]

Aim of the research is to find out the Work value among married and unmarried person's. So investigator selected two groups one is married and other is unmarried persons, both groups have 200persons. In one group has 113 married and other one groups has 87 unmarried persons. The all subjects were randomly selected. Data were collected from Ahmadabad district. Scale was use for data collection is personal datasheet and Work value scale developed by super (1970) and this scale was translated into Gujarati by Jalawadiya (2002), and data were analysis by „t" test. Result show, There is no significant mean difference of Work value between married and unmarried persons. There is no significant difference of the Work value of joint and nuclear families. The high income persons work value is better than the low incomes.

[1]Dept. of Psychology, SP University, Vallabh VidhyaNagar 388120, Gujarat

Grateful Acknowledgements
The Authors

A. K. Chaudhary
Ahir Archana P
Akanksha Sharma
Ali Asgari
Alpesh B. Kotar
Ankit P. Patel
Chaudhary A.K
Chauhan Ajay.J
Deepak Bhardwaj
Deepika Jain
Divya Ghorawat
Dr. Arvindgiri K. Aparnath
Dr. D. J. Bhatt
Dr. D. S. Charan
Dr. Javnika Sheth
Dr. Jayesh N. Bhalala
Dr. Milan P. Patel
Dr. N. D. Mundada
Dr. Pankaj S. Suvera
Dr. Pubalin Dash
Dr. Ravindra Kumar
Dr. Rita Karmakar
Dr. S. M. Makvana
Dr. Shashi Kala Singh
Dr. Thiyam Kiran Singh
Dr. V.D. Kasture
Gandharva R. Joshi
Garima Gupta
Jain N
Jashvantbhai Devda
Kachchhi Parvati K
Kartiki Porwal
Kiranben Vaghela
Kothival Krishna P
Maniya Anil A
Manoochehr Azkhosh

Mohit M. Pandya
Mr. Ankur D. Chaudhari
Mr. Bhavesh G. Gopani
Mr. Pravin A Baviskar
Mr. Rajendra M. Parmar
Mr. Rajput Kiransinh
Natwarsinh
Mr. Sandipkumar N. Patel
Ms. Hiral Y. Suthar
Ms. Niharika Saini
Mukesh B Bhatt
Mukesh C. Rathwa
Neha Nafis
Nilaben M. Borad
Nitin R. Korat
Pancholi Haresh
Patel Hiren
Patel Priyanka D
Pooja Verma
Prof. Anjali Ghosh
Prof. J. Mahato
Ramesh O. Prajapati
Rathod Chirag R
Ravina Madan
Ruchi Sundriyal
Ruhanshi Mathur
Sanjeev Tripathi
Shaik Ali
Shilpa Chouhan
Shyam Mehta
Sonalba G. Parmar
Subhash Meena
Sunil S. Jadav
Urvashi Sharma
Vikas K. Rohit
Yoseph Shumi Robi

Grateful Acknowledgements
The Editors

Dr. D. J. Bhatt	Dr. Thiyam Kiran Singh
Dr. John Michel Raj. S	Dr. Milan P. Patel
Dr. Tarni Jee	Mr. Yoseph Shumi Robi
Prof. C.R. Mukundan	Dr. Priyanka Kacker
Prof. M. V. R Raju,	Dr. Ali Asgari
Dr. Samir J. Patel	Dr. Ajay K. Chaudhary
Dr. Ashvin B. Jansari	Dr. Mahipat Shinh Chavada
Dr. Savita Vaghela	Dr. Navin Patel
Prof. Akbar Husain	Dr. M. G. Mansuri
Dr. Sangita Pathak	Dr. Bharat S. Trivedi
Dr. Amrita Panda	Lexi Lynn Whitson
Dr. Shashi Kala Singh	Dr. Rūta Gudmonaitė
Dr. Pankaj Suvera	Dr. Mark Javeth
Dr. Subhas Sharma	Dr. S. T. Janetius
Dr. Raju. S	Dr. Vincent A. Parnabas
Dr. Yogesh Jogasan	Deepti Puranik (Shah)
Dr. Ravindra Kumar	Dr. Santosh Kumar Behera
Dr. Karsan Chothani	Heena Khan
Dr. Shailesh Raval	Nayanika Singh
Dr. R. B. Rabari	Dr. Soma Sahu
	Dr. Varghese Paul K

Term Words

Academic Anxiety Scale for children-31
Academic Stress Questionnaire (ASQ)-67
Adjustment Inventory (RAI)-11
Adjustment Inventory-7, 14
Adjustment Questionnaire Developed by D. J. Bhatt (1994)-10
Anxiety scale by Dr. V. P Sharma (1971)-18
Bell (1905)-3, 4
Bell Adjustment Inventory-9, 12
Bhatt, (1994)-3, 4
Colour Preference Test-58
Depression scale-66
Dimensional Personality Inventory-60
Dr. Yashvirsinh Scale-19
Emotional competence scale-34
Emotional intelligence scale-35, 36
Emotional Intelligence Test-39
Emotional Maturity Scale-60
Emotional quotient scale-57
Eysenck's Personality Test-58
Health Care Awareness Inventory-7
Health Questionnaire-12
IQ test-22
Job Descriptive Index-63
Leadership style scale-47
Life Satisfaction Scale-68
Marital adjustment inventory-6, 54
Mental health Battery" (MHB)-62
Mental Health Inventory-54
Mental Health Scale-52, 55
Mental health tools-49, 50
MHI (Mental Health Inventory)-53
NEO-Five Factor Inventory-61
Psychological Well-Being Scale-6
Role Efficacy Scale-33
Scale of Insecurity-46
Stress Management Questionnaire (SMQ)-64
Stress Management Scale (SMS)-65
Well-being scale-71
Women social freedom scale-14
Work value scale-77

www.ingramcontent.com/pod-product-compliance
Lightning Source LLC
Chambersburg PA
CBHW060520290526
45791CB00001B/468

* 9 7 8 1 5 1 6 9 5 7 5 6 9 *